Praise for PleaseFireMe.com

"PleaseFire Me is a really funny, bitchy co-worker"
—*The L Magazine*

"If you're too chicken to quit, check out PleaseFireMe where people beg to be fired."
—NBCChicago.com

"An FMyLife-esque venting ground for the malemployed . . . Wallow in schadenfreude at PleaseFireMe.com."
—Thrillist

"At a time when nearly 17 percent of the U.S. labor force can't find full-time (or any!) work . . . PleaseFireMe is not the most sensitive of titles for a blog."
—*Newsweek*

"Had me guffawing with laughter . . . you will realize you are not alone. It's stuff like this, the universality of it, that makes a powerful and hilarious book."
—Sheila O'Malley, literary blogger named *Wall Street Journal*'s "Best of the Web"

"Since quitting isn't an option the malemployed ask to be fired (not literally, but humorously) at PleaseFireMe . . . It is notable that Karl Rove is one of their many Twitter followers. There's no word on whether he's contributed a post or not. Once upon a time, it would have gone something like: Please Fire Me: I Am Tired of Running This Country into the Ground."
—The Huffington Post

"Hilarious. My favorite to date: Last week, I was accused at work of thinking. Please fire me, indeed!" —Times & Transcript

"Your boss is illiterate, your co-worker eats her own hair—whine it all out on PleaseFireMe." —Details.com

"When unemployment gets you down, read PleaseFireMe. Back at work finally? Submit a post." —Unemploymentality

"How to be less awkward: Read PleaseFireMe and be happy your job isn't that bad." —Smart Pretty and Awkward

"Really digging PleaseFireMe . . . As any savvy assistant knows, being fired is way better than quitting, because then you get unemployment benefits!" —Save the Assistants

"It's become almost taboo to complain about your job, since you know you're lucky to have one. That doesn't mean people who were unhappy at work have suddenly become happy. No, these people need an anonymous forum to release their bottled-up frustrations. Fortunately, there is one . . .

"PleaseFireMe made me realize how cathartic it is to hear other people complain about their jobs."
—Marketplace, American Public Media

"Colorful . . . relatable . . . If your boss invites you to meetings to discuss the fact that there are too many meetings, or refers to your 'bereavement and unpaid family leave' as 'vacation,' then PleaseFireMe is the site where you can let the world know."
—Industry Market Trends

PLEASE FIRE ME

Posts from the **Revolting** Workplace

Adam Chromy and Jill Morris
with Johnny McNulty

CITADEL PRESS
Kensington Publishing Corp.
www.kensingtonbooks.com

CITADEL PRESS BOOKS are published by

Kensington Publishing Corp.
119 West 40th Street
New York, NY 10018

All Kensington titles, imprints, and distributed lines are available at special quantity discounts for bulk purchases for sales promotions, premiums, fund-raising, educational, or institutional use. Special book excerpts or customized printings can also be created to fit specific needs. For details, write or phone the office of the Kensington special sales manager: Kensington Publishing Corp., 119 West 40th Street, New York, NY 10018, attn: Special Sales Department; phone 1-800-221-2647.

CITADEL PRESS and the Citadel logo are Reg. U.S. Pat. & TM Off.

First printing: May 2011

10 9 8 7 6 5 4 3 2 1

Printed in the United States of America
CIP data is available.

ISBN-13: 978-0-8065-3443-5
ISBN-10: 0-8065-3443-5

Dedicated to everyone hooking up at work.

*Your love, lust, and furtive stairway trysts
are a much needed affront to company tyranny.*

Contents

Preamble to the Revolution

The workers have posted! And we hear you.

Since we launched PleaseFireMe.com as a venue for workplace venting, we have received thousands of cries of help from every level of worker—including your boss—becoming the world's largest repository of proletarian misery outside of Detroit.

After hearing thousands and thousands of cries for help, we realized two things: First, that employment in this country is not only getting less numerous; it's getting worse.

How do we know? Corporations always do what makes them the most profit. In our capitalist system, profit is the only reason corporations exist—and cheap labor is more profitable than happy workers. If the boss trying to tell you that the new espresso pod machine is a "perk" says otherwise, remember that (a) you could have bought that with a raise and (b) you're still getting killed by Chinese competitors.

So the highest-level executives have taken Henry Ford's idea of the low-cost, interchangeable parts and applied it to labor (or "labour" if you're reading this in the UK—where you may be more used to tyranny). One-of-a-kind parts are expensive to make and replace, and the same is true for the unique people that would be necessary to fill interesting jobs. Take a baker who gets up every morning to painstakingly bake all the bread for a bakery. That baker has all the different skills for making all kinds of breads and desserts, not to mention running a kitchen, buying ingredients, and singing charming Old Country songs while flinging dough around. Even if they make the same amount, he or she has got to be happier, *ceteris paribus,* than the poor sap who presses the ON button on a modern bread oven. Since that sap has no skills, he was also just fired for being five minutes late (because he was up late drinking and wondering where the adventure has gone in the world).

Too simple of an analogy for you, College Boy/Girl? Too manual labor? What about sales? Good salespeople were charmers that hit the road, selling products, sometimes door to door while enjoying face time with fellow man and occasional lonely housewife. Good salespeople, though, were expensive to maintain. Now there's boiler rooms with low-wage order-takers to read scripts and run credit card charges. These "customer call centers" can be run even cheaper in other countries. Stockbrokers? E*Trade. Technical service? Call centers again. Journalists? Sure there are some huge journo-gurus like Malcom Gladwell and Thomas Friedman and . . . uh . . . ? Why pay a journalist when you can link an AP story, or cut out the middleman of reporting entirely and start a news network to present whatever

blond-narrated view of reality you wished were true? Even doc-
tors have been reduced to underpaid prescription dispensers.

We call these jobs that have been reduced to the lowest level
of interest or functionality *malemployment,* and the workers in
these jobs *the malemployed*— The malemployment numbers are
rising as companies constantly look to lower costs by cutting all
expenses and eyeing each intriguing or desirable job description
as fat in need of trimming. (Tip: Don't act too happy at work; you
will attract unwanted attention.)

Sure, that's a bit of a simplification—but look around you
at the layers of management and HR rules and the dozens and
dozens of multinationals that employ dozens and dozens of thousands of people. Even Goldman Sachs has many many times
the number of employees they did in 1990—you think all those
bankers are going to be able to each have rewarding careers?

But what about the top earners? CEOs and superstars are
making more than ever! Ironically, that's part of it. It is true that
those who climb to or began at the top are getting richer than
ever. And the CEOs who can get to the top of this lopsided labor pyramid are making awesome money, let's be clear. But what
happens when the top percent keep making more of their money
by streamlining their employees lives into frustrating, unreward-
ing time-sucks? Revolution.

That's right, kids, you should have been paying more attention in history class. Revolutions don't just happen to other people
in far-off exotic lands. They can and have happened here. In fact,
we have had a revolutionary war and a civil war in America in
just over a couple hundred years, not to mention an industrial
revolution, a civil rights movement, and feminism and its hotter

sister the sexual revolution. Radical change does happen even here in the US of A (and sometimes it even gets you laid!).

Corporations will *not* willingly reverse the trend of spreading malemployment. We continue to become a more equal opportunity nation, but more of those opportunities will suck. The average working salary is in real terms still at 1970s levels. The government dares not interfere in the fiefdom of its legislators' underwriters. We must unite and fight to overthrow the system to make our lives worth living.

We have read your posts and published them in this book to motivate us all for the battles ahead. As you embark on this journey of hilarious spite, frustration, anger, schadenfreude, shattered dreams, and sadness, keep in mind that for every post, there is an entire career of hopeless toil. For every post here there are dozens unprinted from the site, and for every post here there are hundreds alike out there somewhere, in the mysterious non-Internet.

We have scoured the libraries and history books (and/or skimmed some Wikipedia posts) to find the best revolutionary tactics to share with you. We've focused on the boozier revolutions over the very inspirational but slightly less fun Gandhi-type hunger strikes—if the revolution were boring you might as well stay in your job, right? Read on, join in, and spread the word. This book is our manifesto, and Please Fire Me (PFM!) is our rally cry!

PLEASE
FIRE ME

CHAPTER 1
Powerpoint the Finger at Them

An informative slideshow to explain your morale is sliding

Thank you for meeting us in this abandoned office space. Welcome to the Underground. Quickly, now! Someone get the lights! Go! Go! Go! We have a life-or-death Power-Point presentation to get to! Also, you can't keep your yogurt in the fridge because we're squatting.

Each slide features a cry for help submitted to our popular website PleaseFireMe.com, the only place where mistreated workers may "Submit if they can't quit." As we mentioned on the payphone when we spoke to you through our top-secret voice-changing device, we're here from the Please Fire Me Revolution. To make this meeting less creepy, we will speak to you with our real voice—not the evil robot voice that had to repeat everything because you said it was hard to understand. Please pay attention: we've responded to each PFM submission with

100 percent accurate research and material that you may find useful as the Revolution progresses.

Please sit back for about ten minutes while we figure out how to set up the video projector. I hope we have the right adapter cord. Someone please hum to make it less uncomfortable in here. Just give us a second. I think we have this thing working. You'll know it's working if you see pie charts.

Famous Lines in Quitting

I will demean neither myself nor Chanel No. 5 by continuing
to sell to you suburban . . . Neanderthals!

—Nolan Harte, Nordstrom's salesman, 2004

PowerPoint

the Finger

at Them

Please fire me. My boss once said in a meeting with all her staff: "I don't want anyone to assume that they have any clue about what they're doing."

Percentage of Staff Believed to Know Something

■ Know Nothing

□ Know Something

Please fire me. I was talking to my boss a couple of weeks ago and in the middle of the conversation he said, "This isn't very interesting to me."

Topics That Hold Boss's Attention

•New racquetball club
•Sexy paper towel commercial
•Breads
•Old racquetball club
•How shitty your cell phone is

Topics That Don't Hold Boss's Attention

•Dream you had about local electronics store
•Your sleeping schedule
•Your stalker
•How no one got paid this month
•It's a girl

PFM - Unappreciated

Please fire me. You are a moron, and no one wants to hear about the "grizz that almost got you" anymore.

Reasons Why Staff, Grizzes Hate Your Boss

Staff

Grizzes

Recently discovered Twitter

Litters

Scared off tasty deer

Didn't like *Grizzly Man*

Wears US Open socks every day

Left great-smelling food tied to tree all week

Leaves radio on full blast

Acts as "office matchmaker"

Tells sexist jokes

Parked next to favorite tree

Took creepy pics of kids at office picnic

Took creepy pics of cubs foraging at picnic

PFM - The Bear Missed

Please fire me. I work in a retouching department, and while editing panties and lingerie, I was asked to remove any visible vaginas.

GUESS THAT UNBEARABLE CAREER: VAGINA ERASER

a) *Panty and Lingerie Monthly* photo-retouching artist
b) Georgia O'Keeffe Children's Museum censor
c) *Invisible Vaginas Monthly* photo retouching artist
d) Transsexual-Up-Skirts.com photo-retouching artist
e) Hilton family portrait retouching artist
f) Mattel Barbie designer

PFM - Degrading

IF YOU GUESSED "C,"
CONGRATULATIONS.

YOU ARE THE VERY
BEST AND WE HAVE
JUST THE PUBLIC
DOMAIN TROPHY TO
PROVE IT.

PFM – Degrading, cont'd

Please fire me. Sometimes on my lunch break I drive to the park and cry.

Signs You May Be Malemployed

❏ Your boss only remembers your name when he's mad at you.

❏ You've seen a co-worker's genitalia. No exceptions.

❏ Your co-worker conducts personal calls with the volume and emotion of a right-wing talk radio host.

❏ Your co-workers often speak in a shared "funny" voice. Everyone else thinks it's hilarious. If guns could kill jokes, you would buy one just to shoot it, despite your strong anti-gun feelings. (Your brother was killed in a hunting accident.)

❏ You, your company, and the customers have a hate-hate-hate relationship.

PFM – Work Environment

Please fire me. I work for family.

PFM – Mommy/Daddy Issues

How to Live with Yourself If You Work for Your Parents

❖Remember a time when you could yell "You're not the boss of me!" before slamming your door.

❖Tell yourself it's only temporary until you quit or one of them dies—then a promotion is possible!

❖Go crazy after hours!

❖Hit on the boss's stepchildren, if any exist.

❖Steal their operating model, then ruthlessly put them out of business.

PFM – Mommy/Daddy Issues, cont'd

Please fire me. I have four empty-headed bosses who lie to us and cause us to lose jobs. The GM (married) brings whores into the office and hires them temporarily.

PFM – Whores

Prostitute Co-Worker

Pros(titues)	Cons
Finally someone to take smoke breaks with	Stray wig hairs everywhere
Nice boob action going on	Constantly asking how to use fax machine
Something for you to complain about	Makes $40 an hour more than you
Impossible to look slutty in comparison	Staining all the chairs
Has fake eyelashes in case you forget	Eats your bananas out of the fridge and spits into garbage instead of swallowing

PFM – Whores, cont'd

Please fire me. Today I Photoshopped eight small children into a sardine can.

Pollock's *Blue Poles, Kids,* Photoshop Work Thing

PFM - Graphic Design

Please fire me. I am dressed like a smoothie.

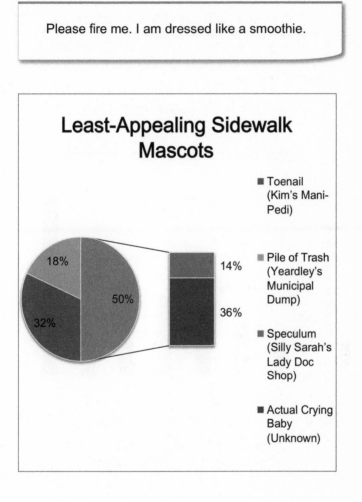

PFM - Attire

Please fire me. One of my students wrote that she wants to go to graduate school and get her "doctric." She is a senior in college and will teach elementary children next year.

Least Useful Advanced Degrees

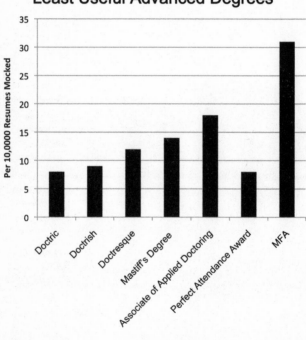

PFM – No Intelligent Life

Please fire me. Last week a co-worker asked me, "What day is Black History Month?"

"What day is Black History Month?"

Acceptable Answers:

1."If you have to ask, you weren't invited."
2."February 1st. Also the 2nd, and the 3rd…"
3."Oh it was yesterday, sorry."
4."It's February. You know, the shortest month of the year? Because apparently America can only half pay attention to African-Americans for 28 days, not the full 30. Now I'm angry. Stop asking me questions."

PFM – Ignorant Co-Worker

Please fire me. My boss refers to everyone as "Ol'
Boy" — clients, employees, even the mail lady —
and expects us to know whom he's talking about.

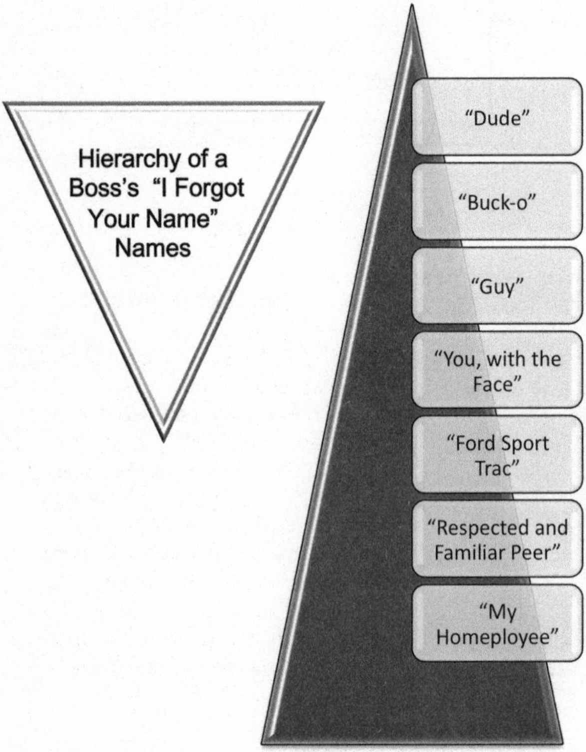

Hierarchy of a
Boss's "I Forgot
Your Name"
Names

"Dude"

"Buck-o"

"Guy"

"You, with the
Face"

"Ford Sport
Trac"

"Respected and
Familiar Peer"

"My
Homeployee"

PFM – Boss Suffering from Employneesia (see page 86)

Please fire me. I have an extensive knowledge of women's blouses and old-lady tea hats. I am a 23-year-old male

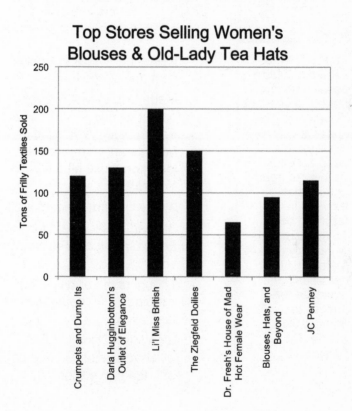

PFM – Too many blouses

Spotlight on Cloris Leachman!

Please fire me. I share a cubicle despite the fact I have 20 years of experience. The space is way too small for two people. I think calves are treated better when they are in veal-fattening pens. To make matters worse, my cube-mate surfs the net all day and searches for images of 85-year-old actress Cloris Leachman.

- Keeps her Oscar in freezer so it doesn't go bad
- Made love to Mel Brooks on set of *Young Frankenstein*, who said of her bosom, "A man could leach on those all day! Yowza!"
- Always returns voicemails
- Badass replacement for Edna Garrett on "Facts of Life"
- Thoughts of her only thing keeping 1,200 depressed fans alive
- Won Miss Chicago 1946 with sad tale of growing up with the name Cloris

PFM – Cloris Leachman Only Thing to Live for Anymore

Please fire me. Our HR girl overheard me describing the plot of *The Road* to a co-worker. You know, the book about survivors of nuclear Armageddon who are being chased across a deserted America by anarchist cannibals. She asked, "Was that based on a true story?"

10 Reasons Your Co-Worker Thinks *The Road* Is Nonfiction...

PFM – Fellow Worker Too Dumb

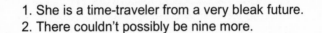

1. She is a time-traveler from a very bleak future.
2. There couldn't possibly be nine more.

PFM – Fellow Worker Too Dumb, cont'd

Please fire me. The dude I sit next to makes a joke about TPS reports every single day.

A Word About *Office Space*...

- *Office Space* is a funny movie. Heck, it may even be the best *Office Space*-esque movie out there. However, we have all seen it—all of us—at least twice. We know that they ask for a lot of TPS reports. It's very funny when those paid actors did it in that low-budget indie picture. It was especially funny because no one had ever done it before.

- Do you know when *Office Space* is the funniest? When you're not at work thinking about how you labor in exactly the same sort of soul-erasing laboratory rat maze of a company as the fictional Initech. Especially because you don't have a deus ex machina in the form of a possibly handicapped ingrate who will burn your company to the ground. And for all its faults, at least no one at Initech sits around quoting *Office Space*.

- Ironically, people who quote *Office Space* in the office always end up sounding like that "Oh-face" guy from *Office Space*. Oh! Oh! Oh! Oh no, it just happened to us.

- Even if you and your co-workers recite the whole script every day, you'll still be at your job and not having sex with Jennifer Aniston.

PFM –Get Off the Mike (Judge)

Please fire me. I got an email from a co-worker asking if eating cotton candy elicits as much happiness as riding on a Ferris wheel.

Metric Funs Over Time!!!

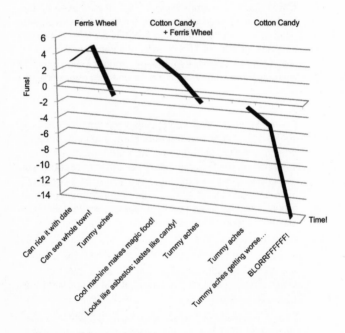

PFM – Emails! ☺

Please fire me. I was invited to a meeting to discuss the fact that there are too many meetings.

Is this a sign of the Apocalypse? Would it be appropriate to wear a tinfoil hat to such a meeting in order to avoid vanishing from this plane of existence into the paradoxical universe of oxymoron-land?

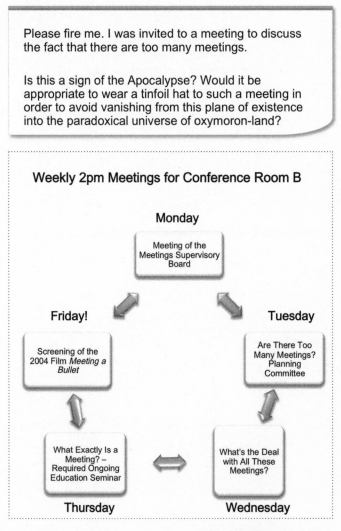

Weekly 2pm Meetings for Conference Room B

Monday

Meeting of the Meetings Supervisory Board

Friday!

Screening of the 2004 Film *Meeting a Bullet*

Tuesday

Are There Too Many Meetings? Planning Committee

Thursday

What Exactly Is a Meeting? – Required Ongoing Education Seminar

Wednesday

What's the Deal with All These Meetings?

PFM –Meeting the Limit

CHAPTER 2
A Mind Is a Terrible Thing to Copy and Paste

The University of Oxfired offers continued education for the miserable

Thank you for meeting us at the outlet coffee mug store Mug Shots. Please take this university literature. You have a crappy job, but you can't get a better one without an education, so we're sending you to the University of Oxfired. It is the only institution of learning accredited by the Please Fire Me Revolution.

Many of our nation's most demoralized employees boast Oxfired as their alma mater: data entry specialists, front-desk receptionists, and other occupations that require a stressfully small use of thought yet somehow cause hives. An institution that prides itself on stimulating the underactive brain, Oxfired also teaches the overeducated brain skills to employ at a malemployed job.

You now hold in your hands (don't open it now, Dale!) an acceptance letter, course catalog, and other academic materials. Why should you want to enroll? Their mascot is a whale with a top hat, and you made a promise to your wife you'd endure your job. Not just for her, but for your two Bernese mountain dogs that she made you buy, too.

As leaders of the Revolution, we'll be walking you through your Oxfired packet, asking you to take note of PFM posts that show a frustration with how pointless their job is. As potential recruits, your first mission will be to pretend we're trying to decide what mugs to buy for our Xtreme bowling team Spare No Women or Children.

Famous Lines in Quitting

My, like, genius is like, totally not appreciated here. And like, by the way, Tony, I never like, liked your haircut.

—former Supreme Court Justice John Paul Stevens

The University of Oxfired

Opus combibo, subsisto in schola
("Work sucks, stay in school").

Welcome from the Chancellor

Welcome to the University of Oxfired. Unhappy employees have been matriculating here for over one thousand years. We are the only university equipped to prepare you for a career of mind-numbing tasks. Your journey begins to end here!

The University of Oxfired has three cardinal principles, which we call "The Three A's." They are: Accepting your fate, Adapting to your surroundings, and Avoiding suicide.

From medieval arsenic testers to Renaissance pony euthanizers, all the way up to today's pharmaceutical company anybodies, we've seen humanity at its most debased. When employees hit rock bottom—lying in the gutters of employment, offering their bodies up for a piece of meaningful labor, it is the job of the educational system to pick them up and enroll them before they awake.

Thurston Pendergross founded Oxfired to help his peons cope with the workplace realities of 1009 AD. In those benighted days, the job of picking up manure bare-handed, padding it into a disc and moving it over a few feet was as interesting as a peon could hope for. This was only after being promoted from sub-peon, whose job it is to manually encourage the animals to produce. Pendergross's curriculum helped peons cope, accept, and ultimately not give a shit (a phrase coined on his farm).

My wife, Danika, and I look forward to seeing fresh, dreary faces on campus. Welcome to the Oxfired family. Please do not expect any holiday gifts.

Sincerely,
Percy Montague
Chancellor

Course Catalog

Course Title: Philosophy 145: The Client Wants to Change Everything

Time: Tuesdays 3–7, but professor may decide to go in new direction

Location: College Hall 103 (for now)

Credit: 6 resumé fillers (highly unlikely you will receive full amount)

Course description: Concepts include letting go of everything you worked on, generating enthusiasm for an inferior idea, and biting your tongue without yelping. Everyone is assigned a partner, and will take turns being related to the client and not having to do any work. The exam is a string of indignities that must be endured without screaming.

Prerequisites: Ethics 101: Attaching Your Name to Projects Without Working on Them

Course Title: CompSci 103: Minimizing Internet Windows

Location: pornofactory.com—WHOOPS! Silver Hall room 23 . . . sorry

Time: Wednesdays 2:15 p.m.–2:25 p.m.

Credit: 2 resumé fillers

Course description: Basic concepts in moving mouse to top corner of the screen without panicking. Among the topics covered are smooth transitions, understanding the difference between minimize and maximize, and focusing. This course *Must* be completed before CompSci 104: Minimizing Windows with Key Commands

Prerequisites: "C" or above in CompSci 201: Using Outdated Internet Explorers

---

Famous Lines in Quitting

I'm taking this very crucial ball bearing and going home! Oh, my God! The shrapnel machine! Is anyone Okay? Hello?

I better go.—anonymous

Course Title: Physics 450: The Aerodynamic Properties of Paper

Times: Tuesdays and Thursdays, 5:15 p.m.–6:15 p.m., lab Fridays 12 p.m.–3 p.m.

Location: Office Depot

Credit: 1 resumé filler

Course description: This advanced level course examines crumpled-up paper balls thrown into the trash, as well as folded paper flying shapes. Students will find the weight-to-drag ratios of different stocks of paper, plot the parabolic trajectory of tossed balls at all temperatures and breeze speeds, and test if different folding and crumpling techniques improve performance.

Prerequisites: Physics 101: Napping Without Falling; Physics 230: Throwing Pencils at the Ceiling; Physics 370: How Far Back Can You Lean in Your Chair?

Continuing Education at Oxfired

You do not have to be currently enrolled as a full-time student at the University of Oxfired to enjoy the benefits of our way-too-educated staff. We also allow people who have been hired for a job that do not possess the fully required skills yet to sign up for a class and become a better worker. The registrar found some submissions to the site Please Fire Me to use as examples, to show what classes they could take to improve their efficiency at their amazing jobs!

Famous Lines in Quitting

You can't dump me! I quit!—Susan Angler, Des Moines, IA

Please fire me. Today, I sent an email to my boss explaining a great idea I had on what we could do differently on our weekly reporting. Moments after I sent it, I heard a huge bellow of laughter from her office. The idea was never mentioned again . . .

Recommended Continuing Education Courses

Physics 103—Asking Professors How Quarks Work

Fine Art 273—Showing Your Self-Portrait to Football Players

Urban Studies 431—Offering Well-Meaning Advice to New Yorkers

Religion 120—Cheek Turning

Biology 445—The Evolutionary Bias Toward Assholes

Please fire me. My boss didn't even read the document I have spent years working on. His only comments were "indent" and "add pictures."

Recommended Continuing Education Courses

Classics 234—Prometheus and Other Greek Legends Punished for Working

Microsoft Word 201—Indent and Add Pictures

Philosophy 303—Disappointment Through the Ages

History 234—The Decline and Fall of Workplace Courtesy

Religious Studies 279—At Least God Knows You Did It

Please fire me. To cut down on costs, I am now only allowed to wear gloves when preparing food in front of the customers. All the prep work in the back is to be done sans gloves. Today I had to squeeze out all the juice from a giant can of tuna with my bare hands.

Recommended Continuing Education Courses

Ethics 103—Food Poisoning—When Does It Become Murder?

Biology 531—The Evolution of the Human Gag Reflex

Chemistry 137—Understanding Soap

Philosophy 233—Crawling Inside Your Happy Place

Culinary Arts 241—Tuna Slop Recipes from Provence

The Rise of the Professionaletarian Class

Oxfired has long required that all students master work history before getting their Diplomatificate. Unlike the history of the world, the history of work is a long process of the common man becoming less free, happy, and valuable.

Famous Lines in Quitting

I loaded all the computers with Windows ME. Good luck, assholes.—Raj Chandrasekhar, IT guy

U of O Book and Sweatpants Store

Proudly serving you books and sweatpants for 1,000 years

Books

The Gifted Engine That Shouldn't (Original Classic Edition) by Danny Tooter

Finally re-released in its original hardcover, Tooter's *The Gifted Engine That Shouldn't* is the most inspirational tale of the power of suppression ever told. One of the great characters of children's literature, Gifted Blue Engine has taught generations of children. Bright children learn from Blue that winning makes other kids feel bad. Of course, run-of-the mill brats get to relate to the hero, Dumb Boss Train. The G.B.E. loves efficiently delivering toys, but he's too good at it. However, after Dumb Boss Train tells him, "You cannot...You cannot," he tells himself "I should not... I should not." From that day forth, Gifted Blue Engine carried only as many dollies and teddies as his quota demanded. Ages 22 to 60.
($14.99)

> Please fire me. My boss has asked my department to slow down production so we don't stand out against the other departments who can't keep up with their work.

    WHALE OF A SALE!!!!

Flowers for Algernon by Daniel Keyes

Never has there been a more fun beach read than *Flowers for Algernon*! It tells the upbeat tale of a down-on-his-luck man named Charly who gets smarter day-by-day and then nothing else happens. Trust us! Go read it! It won't remind you of how working has ruined your once-beautiful mind at all.
(~~$20.00~~ $16.00!!!)

> Please fire me. Everything I write for clients comes back with one of the following comments: "Too smart. Please dumb down." Or, "Too funny. Please make this more boring."

U of O Book and Sweatpants Store

Proudly serving you books and sweatpants for 1,000 years

Immobile Beloved: A Novel by Paul Wesley

The novelization of the film *Immobile Beloved* is everything you would expect from a book based on a movie based on an office worker: unforced perfection. Paul Wesley expertly pens the life of Luther Beets, an underutilized assistant, who composes symphonies in GarageBand at his desk because he is bored. The novel focuses on the period in Luther's life when he begins losing his hair and falls in love with a moderately attractive co-worker. Be prepared for literary genius when Luther goes completely bald and finds a better job. However, before the prodigy stopped showing up for work altogether, he addressed three emails to his "immobile beloved." She forwarded them to the entire office.
($8.99)

Immobile Beloved

a classic

(cover redacted by legal dep't due to overly tasteful nudity)

Please fire me. My co-worker just finished a two-hour mandolin solo because he "didn't have anything better to do."

Sweats

Classic "I Go Here" School Name Sweats
($45.00)

Oxfired U Sophisticated Whale Mascot Sweatpants
($50.00)

NEW!!!! Pajama Pants! For after a hard night of studying
($40.00)

Special Feature: History of Malemployment

Malemployment didn't turn into a crisis overnight; it has been creeping into the workplace long before you filled out your first W2 at the AMC 30. Mankind Renaissanced and Enlightened his way out of the Dark Ages only to end up in the Fluorescent Ages. It sucks even more, and there are no castles.

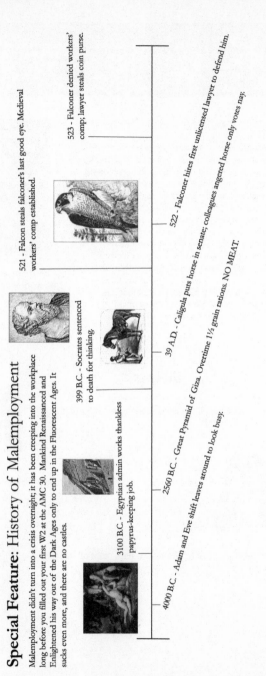

4000 B.C. - Adam and Eve shift leaves around to look busy.

3100 B.C. - Egyptian admin works thankless papyrus-keeping job.

2560 B.C. - Great Pyramid of Giza. Overtime 1½ grain rations. NO MEAT.

399 B.C. - Socrates sentenced to death for thinking.

39 A.D. - Caligula puts horse in senate; colleagues angered horse only votes nay.

521 - Falcon steals falconer's last good eye. Medieval workers' comp established.

522 - Falconer hires first unlicensed lawyer to defend him.

523 - Falconer denied workers' comp; lawyer steals coin purse.

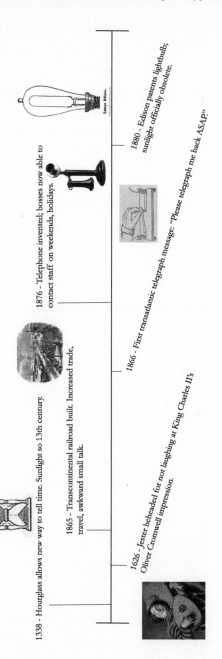

1338 - Hourglass allows new way to tell time. Sunlight so 13th century.

1865 - Transcontinental railroad built. Increased trade, travel, awkward small talk.

1876 - Telephone invented; bosses now able to contact staff on weekends, holidays.

1880 - Edison patents lightbulb; sunlight officially obsolete.

1866 - First transatlantic telegraph message: "Please telegraph me back ASAP."

1626 - Jester beheaded for not laughing at King Charles II's Oliver Cromwell impression.

Please fire me. The only skill I need for my job is knowledge of the alphabet.

How Easily Could You Be Replaced By a Robot?

How much copying and pasting would you say you do per day?

- None—I retype everything like a professional.
- A few hours—But, I'm slow because I don't know them classy shortcut keys.
- 5–8 hours—I don't know how I get out of bed.

Has your boss ever confused you with an intern?

- Never—He's my father.
- Only once—I had to borrow the intern's clothes. Mine had blood on them.
- Every day—At least he tells me to keep up the great intern work.

Do you have to answer the phone?

- No—I just copy and paste things all day.
- Yes—All I do is transfer people to the person they need to talk to.
- Yes—But the only person who calls is my boss's mistress. Then I just transfer her.

How often do you use the copy machine?

- We don't have one. My boss says he only trusts carbon paper.
- A few times per week. Possibly more if it's Peak Copy Season.
- Hourly. I know that machine better than I know myself.

Have you ever spent an entire workday just shredding documents?

- No—HR sold our shredder on Craigslist because of budget cuts, and we were told to just rip documents in half before we throw them away.
- Half a day—Guess which half of that day didn't include suicidal thoughts?
- Yes—I spend every day shredding. They gave me special earplugs.

What kind of benefits do you get?

- My boss told me the "benefit of the doubt" should be enough.
- Health insurance with a $10,000 deductible and no prescription coverage.

- Free lunch every day. Right at noon, a bowl of slop is placed on the break room table. Plates and utensils aren't provided.

Answers

We'll all be replaced by a robot sooner or later.

Please fire me. Last week I was accused at work of thinking.

Thought Crimes in History

Galileo Galilei

Thought his bosses would appreciate him using his nifty "telescope" to find evidence for a heliocentric system, prove the moon was round, discover the rings of Saturn, moons of Jupiter, and sunspots. For some reason, the idea that humans could be wrong about a crucial idea for thousands of years didn't sit well with the Church. Then-CEO Pope Paul V demanded Galileo recall all his discoveries, but they'd already shipped. So, they sentenced the father of modern science to house arrest and damnation, and then accused him of stealing office supplies.

Benjamin Franklin

Thought up a lot of great things: fire departments, civic organizations, lightning rods, electricity, government, musical instruments, etc. Also didn't think to mention he had syphilis before jumping into bed with ladies. Too bad he didn't invent the modern condom.

Eddie Murphy

Thought "party all the time" was a good idea.

Socrates

Thought it wouldn't piss the Athenians off if he taught all their kids to respond to every statement with "but why?" Also thought the Athenians were kidding about the hemlock punch.

Elizabeth Berkley

Thought that playing Nomi Malone in *Showgirls* would show Hollywood she was more than just A.C. Slater's feminist, once caffeine-pill-addicted girlfriend Jessie Spano and launch her into superstardom. Unfortunately, she wound up just showing everybody her tits—and what it'd look like to violently fuck Kyle MacLachlan in a pool.

Kanye West

Thought that if he consistently acted like an arrogant douche-bag, consumers would find him irresistible and he'd sell millions of records and become one of the most famous, richest artists in the world. He was right.

Bernie Madoff

Thought he could use his wealth management business to scam investors out of billions of dollars. The scheme—considered the largest Ponzi scheme in history—was of course busted. The only thing he Madoff with was a 150-year prison sentence.

Susan B. Anthony

Thought that women deserved the right to vote. She led the women's rights movement and traveled all over America and Europe to speak about it. Despite her life of hard work and dedication to the cause, today figures such as Paris Hilton, Kim Kardashian, and Snooki exist.

Ruth Handler

Thought that it "was important to a girl's esteem that she play with a doll with breasts"—and so the Barbie doll was born. It has not been confirmed if the Ken doll was created because someone thought it was important to a girl's esteem that she grows up thinking men just have smooth plastic between their legs.

Oxfired Insists on the Classics: Myth of Bizyphus

An incredibly deep essay by Al Camus, III

Bizyphus & His Total Rock Block

There is but one serious question for the working man and that is of self-termination. Let us look at the classic story the Myth of Bizyphus.

Bizyphus was condemned by his co-workers to absentmindedly work to classic rock music from 9 to 5. He didn't know why they listened to it. The programming of CROQ, "The Crocadillo," quite frankly, seemed annoying.

To start the day off, Bizyphus listened to *Denise & Buster in the Morning,* famous for their "Breakfast with Badfinger" segment. Their show is six hours. Two hours are prank calls, another two are playing the best of *Denise & Buster,* and the rest are commercials for Six Flags. Then there's the "Daily Four Doors," in which four Doors songs are played in a row. Really, the radio station plays three songs and then repeats one at the end. Bizyphus actually enjoyed the "Five-o'Clock-Songs-About-Sex-Disguised-as-Food Block." However, it makes him too aroused to move from his chair, which, in turn, makes him a miserable, shameful man.

He didn't particularly care for any of the hits. At best Bizyphus knew the chorus, especially if it was about a lady. He is currently on many online dating sites, if anyone is looking for a man working a shitty job.

Still, the classic rock was part of his job and, in a way, it pushed him through his classic day: answering emails, writing emails, and writing sticky notes to remind himself to write emails. If he suggested they switch to a non-ClearChannel station, like the hip but sometimes awful college station WBOR the Whatever, he would be glared at, and—what's worse—probably have to listen to a co-worker's attempt to be sarcastic.

If Bizyphus is annoyed and frustrated, it is because he is awake. If this myth makes you depressed, you probably either share his fate, or were already depressed to begin with and are looking for an essay to blame it on.

For if one were in Bizyphus's position he may ask, "Should I terminate myself?" the answer would be, of course, no. The musical selections of your co-workers may be annoying, but we as a human race should remind ourselves that despite having bills to pay, we are the ones in control of how we choose to work. We should not be forced to listen to Journey. Because let's face it, the Crocadillo doesn't even play the good, weird Journey like the Whatever does. No, there is but one answer, and it is revolution. Revolution drives out of this world the jobs that cause men like Bizyphus to drown in a sea of Stickies.

Take Home Brain Teasers

You've started a wonderful journey here at University of Oxfired. Of course, it can't really be called school without homework, can it? Take these home with you to complete your studies! These are due Monday; please mail them along with your checks to: Chancellor Montague, P.O. Box 439557, Grand Cayman Island. Your Diplomatificate will be mailed to you once your check clears.

> **Please fire me. I spent two hours preparing a packet that I know my boss won't even look at.**

#1: A Wife, a Mistress, and a Manila Envelope
A boss is traveling with his wife, his mistress, and a small manila envelope with an employee's work in it. He comes to a

river with a small boat. The boat can only support the boss and one woman he is having sex with/item. If the boss leaves the wife alone with the mistress, the wife will befriend the mistress, which is far too dangerous. And if the boss leaves the wife alone with the manila envelope, the wife will open the envelope in an effort to spy on her husband to see who his mistress is.

How can the boss get all three as well as himself safely across the river?

Hint: Given that the wife and mistress would start talking if left alone and the wife no longer has respect for her cheating husband's personal property, there is only one possible first move for the boss.

Solution:

1. The boss takes the wife across the river, and returns empty-handed.
2. The boss takes the mistress across the river and, en route, tells her he can't keep living like this.
3. The boss then grabs the wife and takes her back to the first side of the river, gives her a pretty bracelet he'd originally bought for the mistress, and wishes her a happy anniversary.
4. The boss leaves the wife back on the first side of the river, realizes he's forgotten to pick up Danny from soccer practice, and takes the manila envelope to the other side.
5. On the far bank the boss has a quickie with his mistress and asks her to wait for him at a motel. She leaves, and the boss goes back to the first side.
6. The boss brings the wife back to the second side and never reads the packet because his life is a mess and he is on the verge of a nervous breakdown. Why should he care about some stupid manila envelope?

Please fire me. Today, I was taught by my boss how to scrub a countertop. This is the fourth time my boss has done it this year. I must have INCOMPETENT tattooed on my forehead and be too incompetent to notice.

#2: The Final Counter Wipe-Down

At 9 a.m. when Jan starts working, the counter gets dirty every 30 minutes. (Her boss watches this happen, but doesn't help.) However, the ice cream parlor gets busier at a fixed rate every hour until 1 p.m. and by 1 the counter gets dirty every 15 minutes.

Every hour after 1, until 5, the parlor gets slower at a fixed rate until at 5 p.m. the counter only needs to be cleaned every 40 minutes.

1. What is the rate at which the time to cleaning drops from 9 to 1 and what is the rate it increases from 1 to 5?
2. How long does the counter take to get dirty at 11 a.m.? And again at 3 p.m.?

Hint: Today's most popular ingredient was ground Reese's cups.

Solution:

Jan needs to clean the counter whenever her miserable boss is haunted by the memory of the day he was thrown out of dance school and dumped by his beautiful ex-girlfriend.

Bonus: On days Michelle is the manager, the answers are:

1. From 9 to 1, the counter takes 3 minutes and 45 seconds less to get dirty every hour. From 1 to 5, it takes 6 minutes and 15 seconds longer every hour to get dirty.
2. At 11 a.m. the average time to dirtification is 22 minutes and 30 seconds. At 3 p.m. it takes on average 27 minutes and 30 seconds for the counter to get dirty.

Please fire me. Our boss decided this year's big "PR improvement" project would be to make the floor 100 per-

cent pet friendly. We sell furniture, and I'm now in charge of cleaning litter boxes.

#3: Cats and Felines

Your boss has sent you to a pet store, where you are to pick out and return with an office cat. There are six cats left in two cages. You are facing in the other direction and cannot see.

A pet store worker approaches. She is doable. She says, "The cat on the left has one kitten who loves red yarn and one kitten who scratches people wearing red."

You are wearing a purple poncho.

"The cat on the right has a two-day-old kitten and another kitten that was born on the date of a prime number that is also a movie starring Morgan Freeman, Brad Pitt, and Gwyneth Paltrow," she explains. You hate Gwyneth Paltrow.

"Does either cat have a calico?" you ask.

"I am color-blind," the pet store worker says. "But pick the cat that you think is more likely to have a calico. If she does have a calico, I'll give you $35 and a coupon to Quiznos."

You wonder briefly what your boss was thinking. Your co-workers Amanda, David, and Eddie think she (your boss) is an idiot. Your co-worker Janice is her sister. It is unclear if Janice is an idiot, she is too hot.

Which feline should you pick, or does it not matter?

Hint: It's important to remember Janice is not Harold.

Solution:

It doesn't matter. The pet store worker is lying. She said she is color-blind, but that one kitten on the left likes red yarn and the other kitten would have scratched you if you had not been wearing your purple poncho. If you'd turned around, you would have seen the kittens were in fact man-eating lions. You could have died today.

Advances in Modern Phrenology

Oxfired prides itself on scientific research. While we are a powerful player in many fields, there is one in which no one else even comes close: Phrenology. Oxfired has more Phrenology professors than the rest of the world combined (except Uzbekistan, where it is quite popular). Recent advances in forcep technology have allowed us to research how a person's profession changes their very brain-labels. Below, you will find the most common thoughts all sorts of professionals have, and exactly where in their heads they have it:

Famous Lines in Quitting

I know what you do at home with those quality control recordings. You'll be hearing from my lawyers.

—Tina Hargrove, customer phone assistant

The Mind of a Post-Graduate Cashier

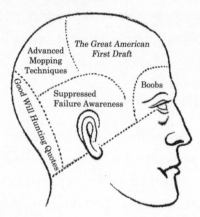

Please fire me. I have a master's degree and work as a cashier. I spend my nights cleaning up bottles of broken wine.

The Mind of a Disgruntled Pet Hospital Receptionist

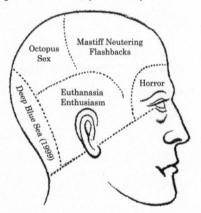

Please fire me. I'm a communication major graduate who has never had any pets, and now I work in a pet hospital as a receptionist. This week alone, I've scheduled thirteen euthanasia appointments, walked through six anal gland expressions, and let the shark in the lobby tank that I feed each morning know the taste of human flesh.

The Mind of a Records Specialist

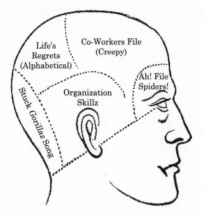

Please fire me. Because no kid ever said, "When I grow up, I want to be a records specialist."

The Mind of a Mystery Employee

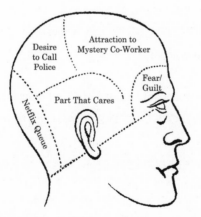

Please fire me. I have been in my job for two years and I still have no idea what the company actually does.

Boss's Language Association Handbook

The *BLA Handbook* is the definitive guide to understanding your boss's butchering of the English language. Recognized by no business schools and still waiting on a publisher.

The Format of the Business Email!

Please fire me. The farther up the chain of command you go, the worse the spelling and grammar in emails. After a certain executive level is reached, punctuation becomes optional. Unless you think your message is really important, then you add lots of punctuation, like: where are we on this????????????? Each question mark increases the importance of the message by a factor of 100 in their minds. Don't even get me started on the poor apostrophe.

Please see below for proper BLA formatted email:

To: ProductSalezForze@googlegroups.com
From: "ULTIMATE BOSS!!!!!" dale.chamberlain@
moneycompany.com

Com t o my tention rctnyl that certain individulLS ANARE MAKIN FUNZAOTS OF SOME OV AR CLINTS PEARANCE.

THIS IS BBBBBBBBBBBAAAAAAAAAAAAAAAAAAAAAAAA
AAAA'd!!!!!!!!!!!!

In concussion 'the client's weight or sexuality is NOT TO BE MADE A SUBJECT OF HUMOR!!!
!!

Reminder to everyone that romorwa is Jnannnnnn's''''

birthday. Plz bringakake.

Peace love and do your jobs,

Boss Steve

This and many of the other, finer points of proper Executive Grammar are explained in the *BLA Handbook*. This new edition includes two new commonly misunderstood Superior Phrases in the ever-popular section "The Mechanicals of Language":

Please fire me. My boss thinks the phrase is "For all intensive purposes."

Please fire me. The president of the company actually misused the word "assertion."

Famous Lines in Quitting

I picked up your daughter from college like you asked. By the way, I quit. I'll have her home by midnight some night this week.—Brad Kendall, stock analyst

CHAPTER 3
Your Work Environment: An Inconvenient Truth

Mapping out the annoyances surrounding you

Thank you for meeting us at this novelty clock store. After the basketball clock stops playing "Let's Get Ready to Rumble" we will begin a deep philosophical discussion. Waiting. Okay. There we go.

Whining about your inescapable environment? Al Gore: Nobel Peace Prize. *The Malemployed:* Chapter 3. Both the malemployed and Mother Earth must withstand unthinkable man-made annoyances. Granted, the natural environment has taken a few for the team, but your personal work environment is unbearable. Every day you are surrounded by motivational posters, the same five pop chart songs, and grotesque-looking co-workers with voices to match. At least nature can sink some ice in retaliation to being pissed off.

Yes, we know you want to retaliate, too. But before you retaliate you must study the lay of the land. Don't worry: you may not be able to escape your work environment, but soon you'll learn how to fight back by being as cold as ice.

An Inconvenient Office Map

Our hidden map proved no match for your sharp mind. When it comes time to recruit, we'll be sure to put you with the others who figured out how to open a fold-out in a paperback book.

Please follow along with this composite drawing and its corresponding legend. You will see forty-three numbers beside various locations in the office. There are forty-three posts in the chapter. This isn't a Brain Teaser from your homework for work; each number corresponds with the numbered post in the chapter. If you need us to repeat that, then your job strain has already killed you and you are obviously the walking dead. Don't worry, we're sure no one at your job will notice unless you laugh at one of their jokes for the first time.

Famous Lines in Quitting

I want everyone in this restaurant to know I never put body fluids in your food. Which is why my co-workers never liked me. Good-bye.—Ken Tully (1993) (Salem, PA, Broccoli Cheese Soup Hut employee)

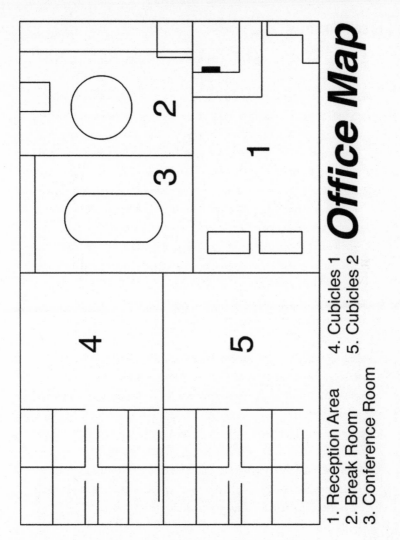

Office Map

1. Reception Area
2. Break Room
3. Conference Room
4. Cubicles 1
5. Cubicles 2

The lay of the land

Break Room

1. Please fire me. My co-worker takes pictures of me in what he considers sexy poses. Me working, stretching, and standing.

2. Please fire me. My department manager goes days on end without talking to me, or even cracking a smile in my direction, then out of nowhere leaves us fun-size candy bars to snack on. The next day she gave us a lecture about eating in the department. We all liked her better when she didn't talk to us.

3. Please fire me. By the looks of it, drinking water from the water cooler makes women pregnant. I just don't have time for a baby now, so I guess I'll start bringing bottled.

4. Please fire me. My co-worker brought in a cake and told us to have a piece. She said she decided to make it because she needed to use the eggs that went bad.

5. Please fire me. My boss hasn't acknowledged my existence in the last six hours, I have nothing to do, and I just got a finger cramp from excessive gchatting.

6. Please fire me. Word got out in my workplace that I am atheistic. Despite having never shared this with any of my co-workers—fearing this very situation—I now endure nonstop attempts to save my soul and make me see the light.

7. Please fire me. I received a lesson on how to use the new break room espresso machine and now possess all the skills of a Starbucks barista.

8. Please fire me. I thought the 365-day calendars with pets and captions were annoying enough. A group of my co-workers, that I have not been invited to join, gathers around at 4 p.m. daily to rate them.

Defining the Revolution

Performance review—n. The annual listing of everyone's personal grudges against each other in a massive attempt to get everyone else fired. *"I'm gonna give that Peters a performance review his grandma will feel."*

Kick Back and Relax

Conference Room

9. Please fire me. I work for a crazy lady who took too many drugs in the 60s.

10. Please fire me. Being $18k under the standard pay rate for my position, I've been expecting a raise the last year and a half. Instead of raises though, my company got us pepperoni pizza they served to us while playing "Eye of the Tiger" to get us excited for our job, and, as a special token of gratitude for our hard work, a $25 gift card to Target.

11. Please fire me. I occasionally have to attend meetings in the conference room where a colleague seduced me. I fell for him. He still works here, too. The women in our lives would not approve.

12. Please fire me. The female co-worker who sits next to me in meetings, whom I do not find attractive, constantly flirts with me. She just dropped her pen on purpose just to watch me bend over and pick it up.

13. Please fire me. I heard my boss use "talk to the hand" three times today.

14. Please fire me. My boss thinks he's a hipster, but he's actually just an aging, balding hippie who can afford hipster clothes.

15. Please fire me. My boss doesn't believe in daily bathing, but instead rolls around in cedar chips nightly. Yes. That's right. Like a hamster. The other day, her dog had puppies. When I inquired about them, she stated that the dog had the puppies in her bed and she still hadn't cleaned up the afterbirth, yet she was still sleeping there.

16. Please fire me. When I eat lunch with my supervisor she moans the whole time. I doubt her cabbage salad tastes that good.

17. Please fire me. My producer blatantly stares at my chest and legs. She's the head of HR.

Defining the Revolution

Furkers—n. Employees who enjoy acting like animals during the workday. *"I caught two furkers in the copy room barking out a memo."*

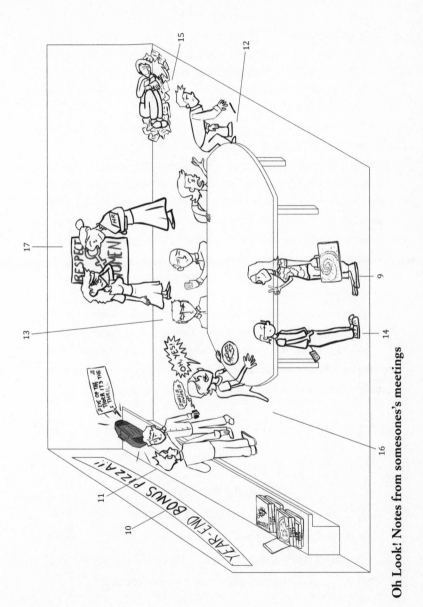

Oh Look! Notes from somesones's meetings

Cubicles

18. Please fire me. My boss digs through our trash cans to see if we are writing notes to each other about her.

19. Please fire me. One co-worker is listening to Kottonmouth Kings, another is listening to 311. I am hearing both simultaneously.

20. Please fire me. Somebody just brought their newborn in and the cooing is making me ill.

21. Please fire me. My co-worker eats Cocoa Krispies every day. Dry. Soon he'll be by to spit bits of them at me when he speaks.

22. Please fire me. The guy I share an office with is head-bobbing to Creed.

23. Please fire me. My boss has been very stressed lately and has taken to eating her own hair. It's gotten to the point where there are now patches of hair missing. Now, this would be fine if it was in the privacy of her own cube, but it happens across the conference table in meetings and, more important, two feet away from me in my own cube.

24. Please fire me. My co-worker breastfeeds her infant at her desk. We share an office.

25. Please fire me. Every day, my co-worker goes for lunchtime walks. He gets extremely sweaty, comes back, and hangs his sweaty T-shirt and socks over our filing cabinet and drawers. After they dry, he wears them again.

26. Please fire me. I work in fashion. If I hear the word "fabulous" one more time, I may have to stab myself in the eye with a pencil.

Defining the Revolution

Ol' boy—n. A person whose name you cannot remember because you do not respect the person as an equal, but whose approval you desperately seek. *"The ol' boy tripped and fell on a cupcake, and it was all over his khakis."*

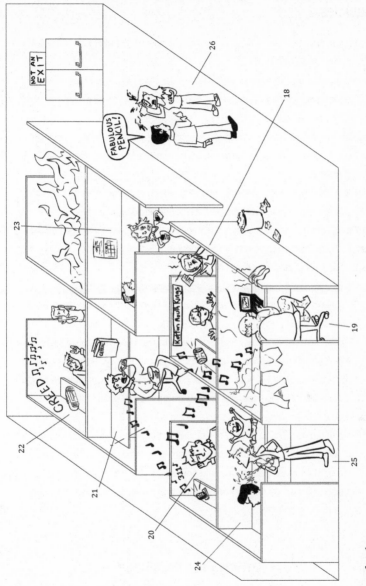

The cool row of cubes

Cubicles 2

27. Please fire me. The co-worker next to me listens to Phish and other jam bands all day.

28. Please fire me. We get emails with subject lines like "Smoking outside: Let's try to avoid burning the building down." Sadly, these emails are not totally unwarranted.

29. Please fire me. One of my cubicle neighbors keeps rotting food under her desk, writes her notes on dirty napkins, and farts as she walks through the office.

30. Please fire me. I wear headphones all day long and my co-worker continues to tell me eight stories a day about her wedding planning.

31. Please fire me. My officemate constantly pops her gum. I tried getting the hint across by expressing how annoying it was that another co-worker pops their gum. She said, "OMG! I know!!!"

32. Please fire me. I can tell when my boss is approaching my desk because I smell her unique fragrance of cigarette smoke, body odor, and fried chicken.

33. Please fire me. There is only one cube in between me and a woman (twenty-five) who will not shut up about her pregnancy. The day I heard her retell seven times how, when, and where she got pregnant in graphic detail was a banner day. She even brought the peed-on test in to show everyone.

34. Please fire me. The couple in our office likes to show very public displays of affection. My cube is right across from theirs and I can see everything. I'm pretty sure someone just got spanked.

35. Please fire me. My co-worker whistles the theme to *Rocky* when he is finally doing something productive.

Defining the Revolution

Slut—n. A co-worker who speaks up about being sexually harassed. "Who hasn't gotten sued by that slut?"

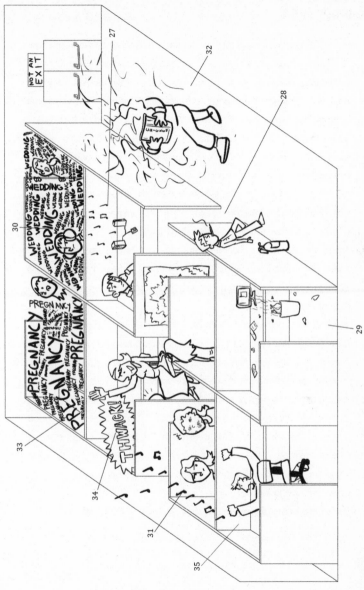

The cool row of cubes

Common Area

36. Please fire me. My receptionist put her nasty fake tooth on the front counter in front of patients while she lip-smackingly ate pancakes and Stromboli at the desk. After the meal, she would suck a big loogie back in her nose and swallow it. Every day. Her replacement randomly tucks his pant legs into his socks, uses the phrase "Well, aren't you the bomb-diggity?" and screeches "WAAAAZZZZUUUP!" You got it: every day.

37. Please fire me. My team leader took a digital picture of everyone's face and pasted it onto an animal cutout. Now each employee is a different animal on the "productivity" board. Whoever does the most work each week gets one step closer to the piece of meat your animal likes to eat that is glued to the other end of the poster. I'm the bison.

38. Please fire me. My co-worker wears short skirts and no underwear. I asked her if she has seen the movie with the actress who uncrosses her legs and is wearing no underwear. She replied no but it sounds like a great movie.

39. Please fire me. You blocked my Gmail so now I have to secretly text people.

40. Please fire me. My boss likes to adjust his underwear while he reads hard copy email in the common area. It's like he does it on purpose to make it more uncomfortable for people in the vicinity.

41. Please fire me. My employer recently stenciled great motivational phrases all over the office walls. "Take responsibility" is nice. "Learn" is a good one, too. "Actively help" really inspires me. I would like to put one up: "Please fire me."

42. Please fire me. Last week, two co-workers were found in the employee bathroom having sex.

43. Please fire me. My boss whistles "Mr. Bojangles" at the urinal.

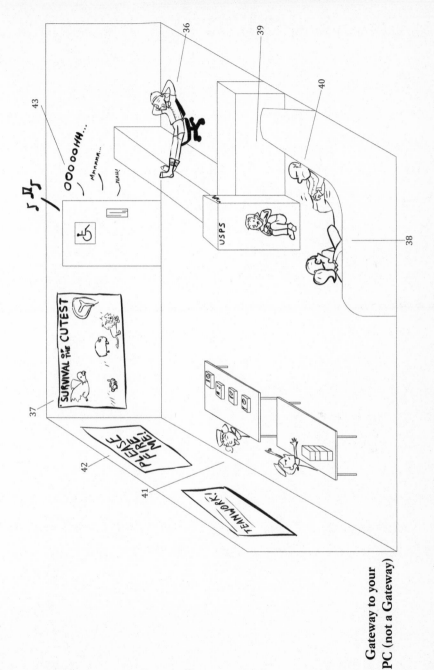

Gateway to your
PC (not a Gateway)

CHAPTER 4
Theirs and Yours: Benefits Handbooks

Like comparing apples and golden-parachute apples

T hank you for meeting us on the top of the Mall of America ferris wheel. Dale, stop rocking! You're going to make us drop these big manila envelopes. They contain your company's benefits: for employees and CEOs.

It's nice up here. But we wanted to make sure we got you a safe distance from your offices, too, because the contents of these envelopes are very disturbing. This thing rocks a lot. Okay, we're just going to be quiet and do our breathing exercises. Read your envelopes. Open them gently please.

Employee Benefits Package

CONTENTS:

1. Afluck™ Budget Insurance Plan
2. Other Things Your HMO Won't Cover
3. Now That's What I Call Annoying!
4. Employee Entertainment Center Welcome
5. Self-Help Pamphlet
6. Intern FAQs

Feels heavy and boring, yet stressful

Acknowledgment and Disclaimer for Employee Benefits Envelope

This is to acknowledge that I have received a copy of my Employee Benefits Envelope. By signing this form, I am disclosing the fact that I am both an employee and a receiver of an envelope labeled Employee Benefits Envelope. At no point in the reading of that past sentence did I forget that:

1. I was an employee

2. I was a recipient of an envelope

3. What the label on the envelope says

4. An array of free pamphlets have replaced the majority of the company's health insurance plan and/or on-duty nurse

Included in the Employee Materials Envelope:

Afluck Budget Insurance Plan

Other Things Your HMO Won't Cover

Now That's What I Call Annoying Vol. 43

Employee Entertainment Center Welcome

Self-Help Pamphlet

New Intern FAQ

Employee Name _____

Employee Signature _____ Date _____

Witness Name _____

Witness Signature _____ Date _____

Afluck Budget Insurance

Afluck™

Afluck provides affordable, quantity health insurance. For more information, please upgrade to Afluck Remedial.

Hair Loss

Please fire me. The president of our company is making the bald men who work here wear toupees.

Male pattern baldness is the only disease covered by the company health plan. All employees are eligible except women. For full-time balding females Afluck recommends Step 1: Wear bandana; Step 2. Pretend to be Gypsy.

This concludes your Afluck benefits.

Retirement Plan

Please fire me. My boss ate all my Pringles after refusing to give me a raise.

The following heart diseases are no longer covered by Afluck: (1) heart disease, (2) heart attacks, (3) heartlessness. For your safety, bosses are required to confiscate all snacks, including, but not limited to: (1) peanuts, (2) chips, (3) sliced apples, (4) Chinese food, (5) salt, (6) grains, (7) baby carrots, (8) Momma Fry's.

Workmen's Compensation

Please fire me. I work for the TSA. I slipped on ice and wound up tearing my MCL and ACL ligaments. Eight months later, I got written up for calling out sick for the three days after it happened.

Afluck provides workmen's compensation to injured full-time employees. Please note that Afluck defines injury as anything worse than the loss of all limbs and/or children. If an employee is deceased due to a safety oversight on our part, the employee should speak with HR between the hours of 2 and 2:10 p.m.

Dental

Please fire me. You don't give me dental, so I hope you like looking at these receding gum lines.

For the benefit of all employees, no employee shall be permitted to smile at work.

Sick Days

Please fire me. My boss snidely told me that she can tell when I'm going to call in sick the next day because I "act sick" the day before. Clearly these are not symptoms and she has caught on to my pathetic ruse to fake illnesses.

If an employee is unable to contract illness during their allotted-vacation half-day, a boss will assist the employee in recovery by any of the following means: (1) challenging them to a fight to see how weak they are, (2) chanting "prove it."

Other Things Your HMO Doesn't Cover

As your HMO, it's our responsibility to make sure you have the facts about the coverage you don't have.

Job Strain

Job Strain is a real problem that attacks those in the worst jobs—high pressure, low control positions. Symptoms include feeling like your heart might explode from stress because every-thing rides on your performance but you're strictly limited by your boss or regulations. Also, heart explosions.

Sleep

Sleep is a problem that affects most employees at some point; however, we do not cover it or allow time off for it. Should it becomes contagious through yawning, you will be quarantined via firing.

> **Please fire me. I sit next to a lady that baby-talks everyone. Needless to say, she is the most talkative in the office.**

Baby Talk

A contagious disease that affects millions of women and emasculated men. Majority of cases are convinced they are ador-able and everyone is delighted by their quirky joie de vivre.

Now That's What I Call Annoying! Vol. 43

You've already heard them blasting out of your obnoxious cube-neighbor's iPod speakers, or yodeled by your boss while

Worse than Volume. 42, which had 13 tracks of "Feliz Navidad"

he tours the floor, but now the best of the worst is in one super compilation! Featuring the music that was so awful, you've still got at least three to four words of the verse and most of the beat stuck in your head! This soulless, tasteless megamix could only be brought to you by the slicked-back-ponytailed execs at Vapid Records and their Now That's What I Call a Cash Cow! series. Now here they are, the songs you've been complaining for: ten workplace anthems and one bonus track for some extra "aaarrgh!" Finally enjoy them at home, or smash them against the wall like you've always fantasized!

1. Please fire me. Instead of paying their employees a reasonable wage, the company I work for invested in making a CD of Broadway musical–style songs about how awesome the company is. They play it to kick off every meeting. *jazz hands*

2. Please fire me. I work for a company that can no longer afford a workspace with individual cubicles; this means that I must share a workspace (a quad if you will) with a man who consistently smells of cheese. Every shirt he wears has pit stains. His favorite musical act is Creed. I do not deserve this.

3. Please fire me. I've been forced to listen to "Bad Romance" on a loop all day.

4. Please fire me. I sit in a tiny room all day, every day, with a girl who blasts Russian techno music from the time she comes in to the time she leaves. We never speak, but there is no one in this world I have more contempt for. I fear that the repetitive, loud, horrible Russian trance music I am forced to listen to every second of every day will cause me to snap. Ten dollars an hour is not worth a murder rap.

5. Please fire me. A low beep has been going off for the past hour, and no one can figure out how to turn it off.

6. Please fire me. I have a co-worker who sings Michael Bublé songs while eating Goldfish crackers. He has conversations with another co-worker about which *Transformers* movie was better, the first or the second. He

also picks his nose at the lunch hour and crashes large jets into the ground on an out-of-date MS flight simulator game on his laptop.

7. Please fire me. The new sales guy will not stop leaning in through my office door and air-guitaring Led Zeppelin, his favorite all-time band.

8. Please fire me. I walked in on my co-workers singing the McDonald's "Gimme that Filet-O-Fish" song.

9. Please fire me! My boss starts off the mornings with Styx's "Come Sail Away." I find myself singing it at random hours of the day. It is the worst song ever.

Now That's What I Call Annoying!

1. "My Sacrifice"—Creed
2. "Bad Romance"—Lady Gaga
3. "9 AM (Opening Theme)"—*Working!* original soundtrack
4. "Suburban Life"—Kottonmouth Kings
5 "Eye of the Tiger"—Survivor
6. "Immigrant Song"—Led Zeppelin
7. "Gimme that Filet-O-Fish"—McDonald's commercial
8 "Save the Last Dance"—Michael Bublé
9. "Beep! Beep! Beep!"—malfunctioning microwave
10. "Tsunami"—Baltic
11. "One Last Breath"—Creed
12. "Come Sail Away"—Styx

Please fire me. My boss gives me the "Always Be Closing" speech from *Glengarry Glen Ross* at least twice a week.

Employee Entertainment Center

Hey. *Employee.* Get in here.

Boy, do we ever have an entertainment center for *You.* Now you'll *Never ever* quit. So just shut up about that for a minute because you could be havin' fun. Livin' life.

Check it out: two VHS tapes, straight from a bin in China-town. Unfortunately, due to budget cuts we could only buy half of each movie. Your boss, great dude, stayed up all night on Windows Media Maker on this. The man aims to please.

Ahem. We close in four minutes. Enjoy!

GlenJerry GlenMaguire

An Excerpt.

Pg. 1

CLOSEUP: EARTH

(Slowly begin zooming out. A satellite whirls by at some fucking point.)

GLENJERRY (V.O.)

Earth . . . fucking look at it. Billions of cock-
suckers . . . all kinds of people . . . and all of
them need real estate. I sell fucking houses.
My name's GlenJerry GlenMaguire . . . and I
don't know how to fucking love . . .

Pg. 18

INT. GLENJERRY'S PERSONAL OFFICE

(GLENJERRY, handsome, is in his fucking office after losing
god-damn everything except his looks. He's on the motherfucking
phone with RODD, his last client: RODD is in his home that is for
sale. Fuck it. We cut back and forth.)

GLENJERRY (yelling)

I WANNA LOOK AT THE MONEY!

RODD

That's what I'm talking about!

GLENJERRY (yelling)

I WANNA LOOK AT THE MONEY!

RODD

All right, GlenJerry. I'll let you sell my $10 million house . . .

GLENJERRY

Fucking fantastic . . .

RODD

. . . and I'm going to go screw my wife who I know how to love . . .

GLENJERRY

. . . I have trouble saying "I love you" . . .

(Dialtone.)

Pg. 27

INT. REAL ESTATE MAIN OFFICE

(GLENJERRY, handsome, wanders through the office after being fired.)

GLENJERRY

(pointing at random people in the office)
Fuck you. Fuck you. Fuck you.

(BETHANY stands up.)

BETHANY (timidly)
Fuck you. I'm coming the fuck with you.

GLENJERRY

Great.
(GLENJERRY steals a fish from the fish tank with his bare fucking hand.)

GLENJERRY

I deserve this.
(BETHANY runs and grabs a bowl, quickly fills it with water, and puts the fish in it.)

Pg. 40

INT. GLENJERRY'S NEW REAL ESTATE COMPANY

(BETHANY and GLENJERRY, handsome, sit in chairs. BETHANY is staring at the window at a family hugging. GLENJERRY, handsome, doesn't have time for that shit.)

> GLENJERRY
>
> All I have is one fucking house and I can't sell it . . .

> BETHANY
>
> I risked everything for you. I'm a single fucking mom and it's the fucking nineties . . .

> GLENJERRY
>
> . . . you bet your ass it is . . .

> BETHANY
>
> . . . do you want to . . .

> GLENJERRY
>
> . . . go out to fucking dinner? Yes, I do.

Pg. 98

INT. BEDROOM

(BETHANY and GLENJERRY, handsome, are laying in bed.)

> BETHANY
>
> What are you fucking thinking?

> GLENJERRY
>
> Fuck.

(BETHANY'S SON fucking runs in.)

Pg. 110

EXT. SUBURBAN STREET

(GLENJERRY is fucking running through the rain. The end of some fucking song that played earlier is playing again.)

Pg. 130

INT. BETHANY'S LIVING ROOM

(There's a bunch of fucking women everywhere, being friends and discussing shit. Doorbell rings. It's GLENJERRY, handsome.)

GLENJERRY
Fuck. I'm looking for my wife.

(BETHANY stands up so he can see her better.)

GLENJERRY
Our real estate company had a big night. We finally sold one cocksucking house. But it wasn't complete because I couldn't share it with you. That's when I realized you won the marriage contest. First prize is a Volvo station wagon. Look outside. Second prize is a set of dishwasher-safe knives. They're in the Volvo. Third prize is you complete me. Get the picture? Only one thing counts in this life: Get me to love you for the rest of our days. A-B-C. A-Always, B-Be, C-Caring. Always be caring. (yelling) ALWAYS BE CARING!

BETHANY (crying)
Shut up. Just shut up. You had me at "fuck."

END.

Defining the Revolution

Malemployment—n. The state of being contracted to do a job that either (a) grossly underutilizes the employee's talents and capabilities or (b) refuses to give proper credit and reward for work rendered. *"I went out seeking employment and got screwed with malemployment."*

Things You Didn't Realize Were Benefits

* Being allowed to feed your dog
* Air
* Legal right to quit if you so choose

Required Morale Boosters

* Mandatory laser tag
* Mandatory picnic
* Mandatory screening of 3-D movie
* Mandatory entry in chili cook-off and mandatory consumption
* Mandatory karaoke duet to "One Sweet Day" by Mariah Carey and Boyz II Men

Where Do You Stand on the Feeding Chain?

How companies and bosses feed their employees says a lot about how much they value those people. Look at these common workplace offerings and see where you rank.

* Free pizza one to four times a month: as valuable as a fifth-grade girls' soccer team.
* Whatever's left in the conference room from the partners' meeting: More valued than yard dog, less valued than inside dog.
* Free Cafeteria: You are a prisoner.
* Fancy Cafeteria: You are a minimum-security prisoner.

Please fire me. You sent out a memo prohibiting excessive drinking at the company party. Seriously . . . the only ray of light this job provided has been put out.

Employees of Alcoholic Companies:
Does Your Company Have a Problem?

"Company" Values

According to surveys forced upon those at happy hour, about one in four employees -- more than 45 million of us -- are products of alcoholic companies.

What's Work Like for Them?

Cold like a beer.

Employees are never thought about by the company, until the company needs somebody to speak for it or bring it a margarita machine for parties.

Consider:

• 65% of all companies would rather be drunk than operating as a business.

• Employees of an alcoholic company are three to four times more likely than the general population to know how to make the margarita salt stick to the glass just right.

• 100% of those hired to make this pamphlet were drunk while writing it.

A Helping Losers Publication

Do Not Lose This Copy, It Will Not Be Replaced

Employees May Be Suppressing Feelings With Trips to the Vending Machine ■

Under the employment of an alcoholic company, a person's need for affirming fist pounds, high fives, and thumbs ups may be ignored. Confusion can lead workers to multiple snack purchases PER DAY. The endless tug-of-war between company and cocktail hour leaves both sides with bruised feelings and burnt hands. This can result in pesky emotions such as:

• **Guilt**. The employee suspects that his boring PowerPoint somehow caused the company's drinking.

• **Anxiety**. Fear of the company forcing it into another game of Russian Roulette at the holiday party can lead employees to not RSVP.

• **Embarrassment**. The employee makes up stories, like the company is too drunk to show for softball against a rival company.

• **Inability to Trust**. The employee doesn't even know what 'Urgent Email' means any more because unless the subject is 'open bar' or 'break room chug,' no one reads it.

• **Anger**. The employee is angry.

Drama, Inc. ■

Over a homemade strawberry wine, leading therapist Dr. Jeremiah Knows explained that there are three common roles that employees take to deal with their wasted companies:

It's not always a fiesta at an alcoholic company.

• **Early Departure Enabler**: Workers curry favor with the alcoholic company by slipping out at 3pm, allowing the company to drink in peace

• **Office Clown**: To distract other workers from the company's problem, clowns shove their unhappiness in a to-do pile, go to the common area and re-create funny moments from movies

• **Embezzler**: This worker acts out, pocketing the company's profits- assuming it would have just blown it on hard lemonade

Warning Signs

The next time you are sober at your unfulfilling job, ask yourself these questions:

- When the clock hits five, does everyone at your company flee?
- Do meetings often devolve into a knife fight over cash bar vs BYOB?
- Is your company email about not drinking at work full of suspicious typos?
- Have any or all of your office birthday parties ended as retirement parties?
- If yes, were any or all of those retirement parties 'Irish Wake' themed?

If yes, are you in denial that your co-worker is dead?

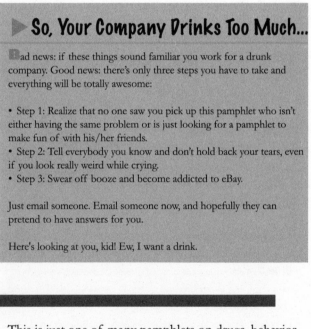

▶ So, Your Company Drinks Too Much...

Bad news: if these things sound familiar you work for a drunk company. Good news: there's only three steps you have to take and everything will be totally awesome:

- Step 1: Realize that no one saw you pick up this pamphlet who isn't either having the same problem or is just looking for a pamphlet to make fun of with his/her friends.
- Step 2: Tell everybody you know and don't hold back your tears, even if you look really weird while crying.
- Step 3: Swear off booze and become addicted to eBay.

Just email someone. Email someone now, and hopefully they can pretend to have answers for you.

Here's looking at you, kid! Ew, I want a drink.

This is just one of many pamphlets on drugs, behavior, and health by Helping Losers Foundation.

Please check us out online at www.helpinglosers.org

New Intern FAQ

Please fire me. My boss just came into my cube and asked me how my internship is going. I am not an intern and never was one for this company.

Welcome New Intern!!!

Common questions our interns ask:

- Wait, why do you think I'm an intern?
- Is this because I cut my own hair?
- Does that mean the intern will be getting my paycheck?
- Why is the intern at my desk now?
- You're just gonna let him throw away my Pizza Town II menu?
- Where are you taking me?
- Is this a broom closet?
- Hello?
- Anybody wanna split a Meaty Pete's from Pizza Town II?
- No?
- As long as we're here, how do I replace staples in the copier?
    A: Ask a real employee, they'll take care of it.
- What the fuck?!

Defining the Revolution

Pi—n. Something nerds argue about in circles. An argument about pi that starts at 3:14:15 p.m. can never end. *"The clock has literally moved 2πr since we started talking about this."*

CEO Benefits Package

CONTENTS:

1. Afluck™ Lordly Insurance Plan
2. Things Hopefully Money Can Cure
3. Luxury Catering Menu

Feels fancy

CEO Materials Disclaimer

Acknowledgment and Disclaimer for CEO Benefits Envelope

This is to acknowledge that I am a CEO and I just received a high five because I'm awesome.

Included in the CEO Materials Envelope:

Afluck Lordly Insurance Plan

Things Hopefully Money Can Cure

Luxury Catering Menu

CEO Name _____

Employee Signature _____ Date _____

Witness Name _____

Witness Signature _____ Date _____

Afluck Lordly Insurance Plan

Welcome back, man! Or lady but probably not. Either way: your skin looks amazing!

Just a reminder: You're covered. Lordly Plan is Full-coverage. It's so full-coverage, there isn't even a real plan because we'll pay for everything. Sore throat? Let us spritz that for ya. Prescription drugs? Just text. First person to contract a rare disease and the only person who knew the cure just died? We know a guy.

Enjoy the rest of your day and whatever your skin is doing, tell it to keep it up!

Things Hopefully Money Can Cure

Employeemnesia

Many bosses suffer from Employeemnesia. Symptoms include calling you generic terms like "buddy," "honey," "you there," or "man." Bosses may develop Employeemnesia after a long struggle with being a Common Asshole.

Defining the Revolution

Package—n. A word learned on *Sex and The City* after a hard day of a successful businesswoman's work. *"It doesn't matter if it's for me, sweetie, I'll sign for your package because I'm Samantha, a god dammit!"*

Work Blindness

A disease known to strike CEOs hardest. Sufferers may have made everyone's life a living hell to get work in on time, but to no avail: these poor souls, when actually confronted with the document, can't even read the introduction. The only cure for work blindness is for an even higher superior to ask for the document. Work Blindness is a close cousin to the disease that prevents presidents from listening to good-looking scientists who have proof the world is about to end.

Defining the Revolution

Harassment—n. When it's not funny enough to be a joke and not good looking, charming, or wealthy enough to be worth it.

"Peter, I had a great time tonight, but I'd like to put you back in the harassment category."

Dé Man's Catering Company

TOP BRASS ADDITIONS

Blackberry Chargers	$140.75
Asian Handjobs	$50.50
$100 Bill	$200.00

KEY PLAYERS FOR YOUR SALAD

Caviar Vinaigrette	Thousands of Private Islands Dressing
Dijon Diamond	Petroleum Vinaigrette
Fat-Free Ranch	Full-Fat Petroleum Vinaigrette

Dé Man Catering Co. is **not** a full service catering company. We only serve upper management, but if you are filthy rich, or can use the card of someone who is, we are happy to do the following events:

Business Breakfast
Business Brunch
Business Meet & Greet/Orgy
Business Lonely Supper
Business Drive-bys
Business Networking Events with Excellent Keynote Speakers

We accept cash, check, credit cards, other peoples'
mortgages, high-class call girls, C.O.D.s, and pictures with celebrities.
"Nous lécherons vos bottes!"

A Luxury Catering Menu Not Meant For You

Nous lécherons vos bottes!

As our motto proudly states, "Nous lécherons vos bottes!" Translation? "We will lick your boots!" Of course, you already knew that, you pharaoh of finance, you king of bling, you caliph of capital.

EXECUTIVE BOSS MENU

Lobster Box Lunches $138.25

Lobster box lunches are flown in thrice daily from Crapoli, a quaint Italian village where peasants have crafted foldable paper lunchboxes since Etruscan times.

Lobster Sandwich	*Lobster on aged Andrew-Jackson and almond bread.*
Lobster Greek Wrap	*Grilled lobster tucked into a warm pita, then caressed for seven minutes. Tomatoes rinsed in water from blowtorch-melted Alaskan glacier, olives stuffed with garlic, lettuce strained while calling your name. Choice of vintage mayonnaise or mayonnaise.*
Lobster Salad	*Organic mixed greens, expensively-seasoned croutons, and lobster sautéed in the tears of a chef (of your choosing). Tossed with Egyptian tongs originally forged for Ramses II and later stolen by Marc Antony.*
Half Lobster/Half Lobster	*Half lobster, half lobster. (Substitutions extra.)*

YOUR EXECUTIVE BIB OPTIONS

- **Classic**: *White plastic with red lobster cartoon*
- **Contemporary**: *Designed by subversive graffiti artist Banksy*
- **Professional**: *Rich burgundy Corinthian leather*
- **Rainbow**: *It's a rainbow*
- **Extreme**: *Full bodysuit of finest French plastic*

CHAPTER 5
Clock-Out! It's Revolution Time!

Glorifying revolutionary heroes like you!

Thank you for meeting us in a parking lot in Tulsa. Do you smell the burning anger? Yes, the asphalt, too, but the anger! Smell the anger! We're here! The Revolution is here! Breathe in the anger, revolutionaries: this is where it began. Okay, everyone stop breathing. We can all agree that smell was more revolting than us.

It wasn't too long ago that the Parking Lot Oaths were delivered over there between the fire hydrant and the median that everyone wrecks into. We won't bore you with what the Tennis Court Oaths are (Dale, we don't care if you know); we're just going to jump right into it. You guys, let's oath it up! Okay everyone: raise your right hand. Now leave it up for the introduction to the oath, keep it up through the oath, and then you can put it back down when we get to our next story of the Revolution.

The Parking Lot Oaths

Scribed on an abornal rock with a Bic

In summer MMVIII, when our troubles were still called the Financial Crisis, and Real Housewives were precisely that; after rousing to the cruel crow of the digital cock, dead tired from their Hours & Beers of forty, and when it was hot out on top of everything, thirty-four employees alive with ideals gathered in the parking lot, shouting at the concrete with these words:

Thus began PFM Revolution!

By the by, one employee was struck by an arseworm wielding a Honda of Our Lord's 1998th year; no injuries to health! Hallelujah!

Beautiful, ain't it? Why did we just say "ain't"? Oh, that must be because we feel a tall tale a'comin'. It's a story we all know and love, but that doesn't mean we can't sit on this fire hydrant and pretend it's a tree stump. Gather round, revolutionaries, for a story about a fella you might know as the working man's hero himself, the one, the only . . . Ronny Fireseed.

The Tall Tale of "Ronny Fireseed"

Ronny Fireseed, Legend

Who was Ronny Fireseed? Well that's a tale for the telling. Ronny Fireseed was a lot of things, but most folks knew him as the CruiseBlue attendant. Ronny was a cabin attendant on the *Hanseatic 9-to-5,* the most miserable cruise ship on the seven seas. His boss was as mean and slow as a fat snake, and his co-workers were lazier than a stoned manatee—but it was the customers who finally caused him to snap.

Ronny's customers were the most miserable old people you ever did see. They paid for a windowless interior stateroom, but they acted like it came with a royal title. To these passengers, attendants were mere servants, and you were allowed to yell at them, insult them, even hit them. Sounds terrible, we know, but people do it all the time—they treat waiters, cashiers, anyone in a service job as less than human.

Ronny was a great cabin attendant, though, and he had a fuse ten miles long before he got mad. Only one woman ever caused him to lose his temper—and it changed the world. One day as the ship was boarding, an old woman and a man were both trying to open their luggage compartments in a narrow hallway. Of course, they got stuck and started yelling at each other. Neither was backing down—they were both important people who had paid for an important steerage cabin. Good old Ronny tried to intervene and asked the old lady to stop pulling for a second. Naturally, like any entitled, self-important customer, she slammed the door into his forehead.

Remember—Ronny was the best of the best, and he had more patience than an entire nunnery. He still didn't get mad—despite a gash to the head and a ruined Friday. Ronny merely left the toxic situation, went to the back of the boat, and didn't see the salty bird again for the entire time the cruise was under way.

Soon they were within sight of port. As we all know from cruises, during docking the passengers aren't allowed to get out of their cabins to retrieve their luggage until the boat is docked and the captain gives the all-clear. Of course, the rules can't apply if you're the only person in the universe—and that's what most customers think of themselves. So that little old lady just got up anyway and started getting her bags out in the rolling seas. Poor Ronny happened to be standing by and told her to sit back down, please.

Well, just like that, the spinster unleashed a monsoon of insults and inappropriate swear words to rain down on Ronny. If there's one thing Ronny doesn't like, it's bad language. So Ronny pulled himself up and said, "Ma'am—you are disrespectful and your attitude and language reflect poorly on your character and morals." By this point, all the passengers had come out into the hall to watch, and they applauded Ronny's calm handling of the situation.

Then Ronny grabbed an eighty-six-ounce frozen margarita from a lush who was watching the action and threw it in the old lady's face. Ronny ran over to the PA system and said he wished "those who weren't total dicks" a pleasant day on the seas, but that all other passengers, staff, and crew should report to the lido deck to screw themselves immediately.

He picked up the now-shivering old woman at arm's length and made an airplane noise as he carried her around the deck. Ronny got a little carried away. Then Ronny noticed the woman's granddaughter was into it and made sweet love to her on a deck chair.

Ronny was losing the support of the crowd now. So he did what any hero would do, he inflated the giant plastic slide that all oceangoing vessels have and slid into Miami's Biscayne Bay. The passengers gathered at the rail to watch Ronny get eaten by sharks. The first fin quickly appeared, but Ronny punched the shark in the face and summoned his mighty strength to jump fifty feet straight out of the ocean! He grabbed the landing skid of a passing helicopter and flipped everyone off as they flew over the boat. It was so plumb awesome that everyone was back on his side, even the old man, and they cheered. He hung there as the helicopter took him all the way back to Fort Lauderdale where his car was parked.

They say that helicopter pilot had just then quit his job baby-sitting traffic reporters, almost like Ronny had unleashed something in his rage that told people "quit your terrible job—or do something about it."

News of Ronny's feats flashed through workplaces like a jackrabbit through a cabbage patch. His name echoed across water coolers, bars, and anywhere workers take breaks. Good ol' Ronny, though, was nagged by a pesky little doubt. He had been sort of a jerk back there, although the sex was a delight. Ronny didn't know, but that granddaughter would never be satisfied by a mortal man again. He was a good person pushed too far by his job, like so many others.

Suddenly Ronny was struck by a big ol' bolt of realization: his dream couldn't just be to give nasty people a taste of the stress and humiliation he had suffered. His dream was to spread a better way of working across America, the fruits of which would be apparent to everyone. Now, there aren't many folks with the willpower that Ronny had, and most have too many responsibilities to quit in a blaze of glory like him. Ronny knew that he could help everyone help themselves by starting a revolution in how companies, employees, and customers treat each other.

So ol' Ronny finally got out of jail for pulling the emergency cruise slide and started tellin' people about the Revolution. He never stopped. Ronny traveled from office to office in his cabin attendant's uniform, which he never took off and never fully dried. Everywhere he went, he planted ethics, tactics, strategies, and a vision of a better Monday-to-Friday. People said he was twenty feet tall and ate nothing but memos, but he was still a man. Everywhere he went, workers started reforming their contract with each other and their company, but they always remembered the funny damp man in tattered rags who inspired them.

Now, big Ronny had a subversive message, but he always had a kind heart. He was a friend to everyone, even the mean bosses and lazy co-workers and balky fax machines and stuck copiers. His hat was a Cool Whip container he used for busking (he played the ukelele), and his favorite book was *The Joy Luck Fight Club* by Amy Palahniuk.

Nowadays, Ronny's disappeared. The task of keeping the Revolution alive falls to those who have heard his tale—folks like you! Some say he retired after he had seen enough green shoots of Revolution to know it would soon grow wild across the land. Some say he led an actual coup in a small island state. Still others say he became pure energy after attaining pure productivity. No matter where he went, there's a little bit of him wherever people are clocking in to the daily limbo, and a lot of him in those who have eaten his knowledge apples.

You don't need to flip everyone off hanging from a helicopter to change your workplace. Below are posts from people who were some of the first to take the Revolution out of Ronny's hands and into their place of malemployment. These were the first-generation revolutionaries, forced to iron on their insignia—made from a printer they hated. Hopefully the people in this chapter, and the ones to come, inspire you to make a change where you work, other than when you come in wearing the same thing as you did the day before and you flip it inside out.

Spreading the Fireseed

Think you can't handle the pressure of being a hero who spreads the word of subversion? These posters didn't seem to think so. And we know that for every revolutionary action, there is an equal and awesome reaction. The proof lies beneath each post, where we detail how the submitter inspired a co-worker to take action, too.

> **Please fire me. The head boss is such a control freak that he doesn't allow paper clips in the office. For Christmas decorations, it was only appropriate that I make a green-and-red paper clip chain.**

> **Please fire me. It is possible to not even work for weeks and our bosses would never know.**

Thanks to this PFM hero's decision to take a six-day weekend, his equally underappreciated cubemate took a month off and wrote a novel. It's called *Cube Thoughts,* a creative nonfiction novel about cubes. He's still waiting to hear back from a few publishers. Fingers crossed! It'd be great if someone finally appreciated your work.

> **Please fire me. On 4/1/10 I exacted my revenge on the ridiculous "bathroom etiquette" signs I stare at every day in the ladies' room. I don't think adults should have to be told not to sprinkle.**

After this brave tinkler stood up and said "I'm a big girl, dammit," workers at an Albuquerque office decided their two-foot wooden "bathroom pass" was past its prime. They took up a fund, hired a guy from Smith's Smithy and Locks, and changed the locks to all the bathrooms.

> **Please fire me. I eat raw cauliflower all day so the smell of my bad breath will keep people from talking to me.**

This anonymous co-worker invented one of the Revolution's most effective tactics: smelling bad. His co-workers were slow to catch on, but once he got close enough to explain without them running away, they formed a cauliflower gang—until they all started turning that cauliflower color. At a private meeting, they voted to diversify their smelly diet. Diversify and spread: The only way a gang can survive. Carry on!

> **Please fire me. I just realized I've gained ten pounds since I've taken my first office job. Today, I threw away the office's free donuts when no one was looking.**

A woman at a branch forty-five minutes away heard tales of the donut ditcher and decided she could take Free-Cupcake Friday no longer. She replaced the cupcakes with apples but put them all in the wrappers of what was once a red velvet treat. Deliciously good work!

> **Please fire me. I make spreadsheets of my favorite snack foods weekly and distribute them to the office—no one even opens them because I title them "EGOFinal-Q1-2010." I've been doing this for about a month and received a compliment from my boss the other day about my "E-G-O Reports."**

This is a PFM classic, so it is no surprise that this malemployed worker eventually inspired an office-wide acceptance of screwing with people through Excel file names. Word is that it's now gone tristate. This spreadsheet attack spread far and wide, and here are the file names to prove it:

- Times_Of_Day_Large_Trucks_Passing_By_vs_Time_Of_Day_Terrible_ Smells_Emerge Near_George/s_Cube.xcl
- Hey_Amanda_How_Are_Things_In_Delaware.xclx
- Remaining_Dreams_In_Office.xclx
- Vending_Machine_Purchases_vs_Daily_Level_Of_Depression.xcl
- People_We_Were_Friends_With_Who_We_All_Forgot.xclx
- Delaware_Is_Fine_Thanks_Gavin_Miss_The_Old_Branch_L_O_L.xclx
- What_Boss_Asked_For_vs_What_Boss_Later_Claimed_She_Asked_Us_ For.xcl

Posters for our Posters

Some posters on PleaseFireMe.com were so inspirational that they came to embody certain principles of the Revolution.

Hoping to pass on the principles more widely, we put out a call to the greatest freelance designers in the world to transform posts into posters. We were upfront about our lack of resources, but they said, "No, let us do our part. This is for Ronny." So hopefully these post posters encourage more posters, and those posters' posts will inspire more posters and then more posters, whose posts will give rise to new posters, and so on. Have you done your part yet?

> Please fire me. I am a recent college graduate with a published thesis on immigration ethics. I am currently working for a payday loan company that preys on people who manage their money poorly. Yesterday, our collections department filed to foreclose on a ninety-three-year-old woman's house because she forgot about her loan. It had been refinanced sixty-four times. That's $5,760 she has given my company. The loan was for $300. After speaking with three different managers, I was told to "take everything she's got" rather than just calling it even.

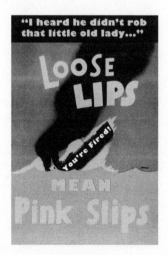

Please fire me. I tried to quit, but my manager told me not to. I said okay. That was five months ago.

Please fire me. If someone asked me whether I would prefer to receive emails from my boss, or take direct hits to the nut-sack, I would choose the direct hits to the nutsack.

Please fire me. My wife went into an unexpected early birth of my first child. When I asked my manager if I could leave work to be with my wife at the hospital he replied, "Well, that's just poor planning on your part. What's more important, your career or your family?"

Daddy, were you at the hospital when I was born?

Defining the Revolution

Maternity leave—n. A vacation given to women after nine months of gaining weight so they can go to fat camp or whatever it is that ladies do to drop about eight pounds. "What do you mean you get nothing out of our relationship? I scored you maternity leave!"

CHAPTER 6
Recruitment

A full report on who to recruit, who to ignore at lunch

T hank you for meeting us. Ooooh . . . a '93 Xerox Stratoscanner. Man, that was when Xerox had style. Today, we're going to talk about how to recruit your Revolutionary army. Everyone take a dossier of potential recruits, a red ink pad, and three red rubber stamps. Based on each PFM submission about how a worker is treated, we will decide their fate: Recruit, Do Not Recruit, or.

People of the Revolution! If you made a photocopy of your face, what would you see? Power. You now possess the power you have to recruit any sad sack you want from your entire office. Anyone. You just have to have a reason to pick them. Like when we picked Dale (excuse us, "Agent Blue Beard") because of his puppy-like eagerness to please.

Everybody have their stamps? Please note: only recruits will be joining the fight. The Do Not Recruits and the Prisses will both be on the sidelines. However, the Prisses will be whining about how much fun and noise you're making. They're the complainers who should have never submitted to Please Fire Me at all.

Now, let's all stop photocopying our butts and then begin. Time is of the essence.

Please fire me. A forty-year-old teammate made an official complaint to our boss because I don't laugh at his jokes. Sadly, that complaint was way funnier than any of his jokes have ever been.

Code name: Silent Hyena
Best quality: Poker face
Hobbies: Going to stand-up comedy shows to read a nice book
Favorite high brow joke: What's the Pope's favorite book? *The Old Man and the See.*
Favorite low brow joke: Dees nuts!
Greatest flaw: Won't laugh at your dumb jokes, either

Please fire me. I totally forgot the receptionist's name and it's super awkward.

Have a feeling there will be a lot of receptionists in this revolution.

Please fire me. While taking notes on the presentation, the person sitting beside me watched a puppy cam.

Oh no! *Not puppies! Anything but adorable puppies!* Mind your own business, tattletale.

Please fire me. Nearby noisemakers were disrupting everyone, and I got in trouble for complaining about people who were just having a "jovial time."

Sorry, people who use the words "Jovial time" are probably a lot more fun than the guy who complains about "nearby noisemakers."

Please fire me. Everyone in my section of the office just had to put up with our co-workers' twenty-minute discussion of total strangers' medical issues, with details like: "Her ovary was the size of a grapefruit."

Code name: Discovery Health
Best quality: Navy Seal–like endurance in horrible conversations
Work style: Extremely gross-details oriented
Eaves range: Can drop eaves from fifty+ feet
Medical training: *House,* seasons 2–6

Please fire me. I hear the copy machine making 1,888,854,2222 copies. When I turn around to see what is going on with our machine, I see my brilliant boss trying to fax through it. FYI: The fax machine is right next to the copy machine, you have used it before and you've worked here for six years.

Instead of emailing Please Fire Me, you should have contacted 9-1-1. Your boss was having a stroke.

Please fire me. I've been working here for a year. Since then, my last two bosses were fired and a high school girl who started last month just got promoted to be my new boss.

Befriend that high school girl— sounds like she's going places.

Please fire me. I am a zoning officer.

Code name: Industrial Use Only

Best quality: Straight to the point

Worst quality: Won't look the other way over your in-office diner

Ideal cubicle square footage: 144

Special skills: Can approve your kitchen nook addition. Also, plays harmonica

Best anecdote: Time he accidentally approved building a mall right around a family home

Please fire me. I had to sit through a meeting at work that involved watching the trailer for *Eclipse* with a bunch of forty-year-old fangirls.

Code name: Team Neither
Strengths: No longer fears prospect of physical torture
Fan fiction: Mike Newton, Monster-Hunter
Family: Left wife after finding Sookie Stackhouse novels in closet
Foreign languages: Spanish, Tween, Tweenopause

Please fire me. I put up birthday decorations in my boss's office after hours because last year I didn't make a big deal for his birthday and he cried.

Code name: Baby sitter
Office committees: Mainly the pity variety
Drawbacks: Can only hang out when boss is napping
Weapons: Streamers, lollies, praise
Weaknesses: Puppy-dog eyes, guilt trips
Powers: Controls boss's tear ducts

Please fire me. I just found out that the rest of my sales team had a lovely time bonding at an extracurricular event that I wasn't invited to. That event was a John Mayer concert.

Is upset about getting to avoid John Mayer concert.

Please fire me. I drove to every Kmart from Santa Barbara to Orange County to find Fisher Price toy nail guns.

Codename: Playskool Fixer
Greatest find: Plastic castle with working hot oil gate defenses
Rolodex: Knows every stock boy in CA
Retirement plan: Wandering around playgrounds collecting toys
eBay user rating: Excellent. "My Cozy Coupe arrived in mint condition!"

Please fire me. I started smoking again just so I'd have an excuse to leave the office for an extra fifteen minutes a day.

Codename: Re-animated Cold Turkey
Strengths: Willpower to quit in the first place
Sacrifices: Willing to shorten life span to make present life bearable
Drawbacks: Always on break when you need her
Resistances: Habit has inured her to cold days smoking outside

The Smoker's Circle

Wherever you find a chimney of noxious, toxic, deadly smoke, there you will find the coolest of your co-workers. Every smokers' circle is a potential hotbed of dissent; away from prying eyes and watchful ears, employees feel free to vent and spew about their place in life. Use this as your recruiting ground and meeting spot—you can always fake the smoking to the people in the office, and it's a lot healthier that way, too. Even life itself may have found its start in "black smokers," vents of toxic chemicals leaking out of the earth's crust at the bottom of the ocean. So it is with your co-workers and the Rebellion.

Please fire me. I am my ex-husband's best friend's assistant.

Involved in shady love triangle/ hate square.

Please fire me. When I asked my co-worker for scissors, he said I wasn't ready for them.

Not ready for scissors.

Please fire me. I work for an extended warranty company with a bunch of adult potheads. They go to the garage of our complex to smoke throughout the day. They flick their cigarettes, still burning, into their ashtray. This sometimes lights it on fire. They don't know how to tell time, so are late every day, if they even show. My supervisor makes 6,000 dollars a month and leaves at 11:00 a.m. for the day to visit a remote-control car racetrack. They spill coffee, food all over, and don't clean up after themselves. They watch movies and play video games all day. One of them even created a cave with his cubicle by adding a sidewall to cover the top. Where am I and who are these people?

Better question: What are you and how does one take your job?

Please fire me. My new senior manager just made me fist-bump him. I'm an accountant . . . I don't do fist bumps.

There will be fist bumps; you can pound on it.

Please fire me. My manager was disgusted at the fact that our security guard urinated on the seat of our only toilet. There were no rubber gloves, so Manager decided to clean it himself. With fire. He poured all sorts of cleaning agents on it: Lysol, Windex, Ajax. None of these products are flammable, apparently. A small group gathered. From the back, someone said, "Here, try this," and handed him a can of WD-40. "Everybody stand back," Manager warned. *Whoosh!* A fireball erupted and all the urine and assorted cleaning agents were vaporized. There are still scorch marks on that toilet seat.

What, exactly, is not awesome about this?

Please fire me. I was in a bad mood and joked that I was low on serotonin today, and one of my co-workers told me that was the most intelligent thing he had heard anyone at our corporate restaurant ever say.

Codename: Sylvia Plath
Strengths: Keeps quiet during meetings, probably wields biting acerbic wit
Weaknesses: Low blood sugar
Favorite appetizer: Cheese-steamed taco poppers
Suspender size: 4 ½

Please fire me. I have to answer the telephone stating my name is Charles Dickens over 200 times a day. Then I have to hear little old ladies jabber about his writings before they make a catalog order.

Codename: Meh Expectations

Least favorite author: Dan Brown. Close second: Charles Dickens.

Best quality: Won't forget to use codename

Worst quality: Uses codename way too much

Special skills: Cursory knowledge of Victorian Era London

Please fire me. I work in a restaurant with a server who talks all the time. Because it has become incessant, we've started a drinking game based on it. Now customers are starting to play.

Codename: Server of Ceremonies

Abilities: Noticing the obvious, making fun of it

Drawbacks: May start a game based on your Dr. Who references

Secrets: Terrified people will notice she talks about rabbits too much

Best quality: Keeps morale high

Worst quality: Keeps everyone drunk

CHAPTER 7
Customer-Training Seminar

Flashing the customer with facts

T hank you for joining us in your office. Please don't blow our cover as customer-service training consultants. Of course, we're not customer-service training consultants, we're the same PFM leaders you know and feel mildly friendly toward. However, we are training-customer consultants. Our cover company specializes in dealing with British customers (limey pricks), so if anyone asks what you learned, say "always offer tea."

We have a series of customer-training flash cards with useful acronyms to help you teach the customer a valuable lesson, in an approachable, customer-unfriendly manner. Some of them are advice, some are mnemonics to help them learn tricky commonsense facts. Some are just there to point out their flaws. Plus, the acronyms will help them remember because they are stupid!

So who can tell us why customers are so hard to handle? That's correct—because they think they're always right. Any other reasons? Idiots, good, they are idiots. Random outbursts of rage, yes that's a common problem. Very good. You guys clearly already have the most important part of training-customers training: a debilitating hatred of the yokels we shake down for profit. Yes, one other reason? Allergic to cats? Dale, you cannot carry that feline . . . thing everywhere. Besides, Chewbaccat obviously hates it when you hold him above your head like that.

If you could pass forward those positive feedback forms you've been filling out, it would really help our cover business. Talking business cards don't pay for themselves, despite what that salesman said. Now, grab a partner and get to flashing some customers!

> Please fire me. I get paid to listen to small children sing show tunes. I always say, "As a voice teacher, I believe that anyone can sing," but that's a lie. Most people cannot even sing a little bit, especially my students. Stop screaming in my ear, kid, and get me an Advil and a gig while you're at it.

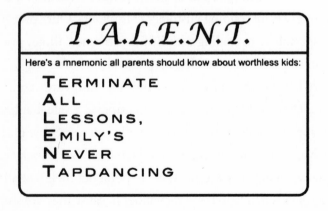

T.A.L.E.N.T.

Here's a mnemonic all parents should know about worthless kids:

TERMINATE
ALL
LESSONS,
EMILY'S
NEVER
TAPDANCING

Please fire me. I just had a phone conversation with a customer who treated me like I was so dumb. He even told me how to spell Jim and then called me Claudia. My name isn't Claudia. Not even close.

S.E.R.V.I.C.E. R.E.P.

Customers should be more polite when talking to a service rep!

STOP   **R**EALLY
EMITTING   **E**XCELLENT
RUDE   **P**ERSONALITIES
VITRIOL
IT'S
CRAMPING
EVERYONE'S

Please fire me. A customer asked me if he went over his limit on his unlimited text message package.

R.O.T.F.L.

This stupid question probably had you ROTFL:

REGRETFULLY
OUR
TEXTS (ARE)
FUCKING
LIMITLESS

Please fire me. A man asked me to leave the unpaid drinks he and his son had on the table so they could go out to smoke. He then asked, "Hey, man, do you have a cigarette?"

By not paying for his drinks in addition to asking for a cigarette, this guy and his son are taking bumming to new levels.

B.U.M.M.I.N.G.

Like bum father, like bum son:

BOTHER
UNEMPLOYED
MARLBORO
MEN
I NSTEAD.
NOW
GIT!

Please fire me. As I served an old man his meal today, he coughed and a huge stream of phlegm landed on my bare forearm.

E.A.R.L.Y. B.I.R.D.S.

The earlier they get up to seize the day, the fewer there are left:

ELDERLY   **B**ODY
ASSHOLES   **I** S
RETCHING   **R**EADY (TO)
LOOGIES: **D**IE
YOUR   **S**OON

Please fire me. I work for a bank. A customer came in and started talking super-fast in Spanish. I told her, "I'm sorry, I don't speak Spanish." She then completely changed her tone and proceeded to yell at me in English, "Why don't you know Spanish? You live in America! You should know how to speak Spanish!"

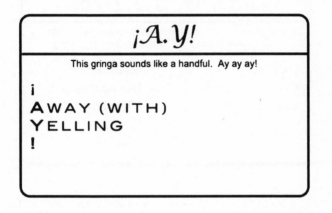

¡A. Y!

This gringa sounds like a handful. Ay ay ay!

¡
AWAY (WITH)
YELLING
!

Please fire me. At the restaurant where I work, I innocently asked my customer, "Would you like to order?" and he answered, "Would you like to lick my asshole?"

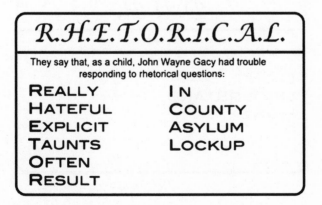

R.H.E.T.O.R.I.C.A.L.

They say that, as a child, John Wayne Gacy had trouble responding to rhetorical questions:

REALLY   IN
HATEFUL   COUNTY
EXPLICIT   ASYLUM
TAUNTS   LOCKUP
OFTEN
RESULT

Please fire me. I work as a waitress on Mackinac Island (between the Upper and Lower Peninsulas of Michigan). I answer questions like: "Is there water all the way around this island?"

L.O.W. T.I.D.E.

Some of the idiots from your neighboring states have intelligence levels that are always at low tide:

LOTS
OF
WISCONSINITES

THINK
ISLANDS
DON'T
EXIST

Please fire me. I work at a bead store and when I answer the phone I include the name of the store, which includes "Bead Store" and one other word. People still ask if we sell beads.

D.U.H.

We're a fucking bead store, duh:

DIDN'T
UNDERSTAND,
HUH?

Please fire me. I told a woman on the phone that I would appreciate it if she would stop yelling at me. She said she would appreciate it if I had half a ****ing brain cell. She was pretty fired up about that pizza.

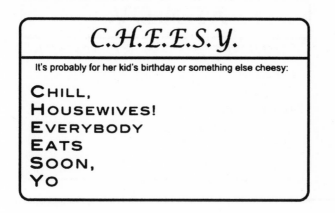

C.H.E.E.S.Y.

It's probably for her kid's birthday or something else cheesy:

**CHILL,
HOUSEWIVES!
EVERYBODY
EATS
SOON,
YO**

Please fire me. I work in fast food and customers like to make up items they never ordered and then ask for them when we bring them their food.

R.I.P.O.F.F.

You don't give your customers free entrees? Man, what a ripoff!

**REMEMBER:
I
PAID
ONLY
FOR
FRIES**

Please fire me. Someone asked me if they could change the sauce on their chicken alfredo to alfredo, instead of meat sauce.

I.T.A.L.Y.

Sometimes big customers bring their little brains to Little Italy:

I TALY
TELEPHONED
AND
LAUGHED (AT)
YOU

Please fire me. A customer came in asking if we have any books on dinosaurs. After answering yes, they asked if there was a dinosaur called a thesaurus.

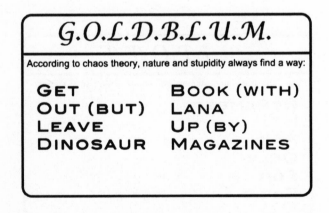

G.O.L.D.B.L.U.M.

According to chaos theory, nature and stupidity always find a way:

GET	**B**OOK (WITH)
OUT (BUT)	**L**ANA
LEAVE	**U**P (BY)
DINOSAUR	**M**AGAZINES

Please fire me. I work in a restaurant. One day, I meet this nice old lady who gives me a hug. Then she says, "Oops, I probably shouldn't be doing that; I have TB."

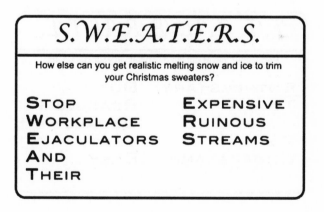

T.B.

Persevere! Maybe one day you'll be as famous as outlaw legend Doc Holliday. He survived many shootouts but died of TB:

**TUBERCULOSIS:
BOO!**

Please fire me. We had to throw away two sweaters at the mall today due to someone jizzing on them.

S.W.E.A.T.E.R.S.

How else can you get realistic melting snow and ice to trim your Christmas sweaters?

**STOP
WORKPLACE
EJACULATORS
AND
THEIR**

**EXPENSIVE
RUINOUS
STREAMS**

Please fire me. Today, an oblivious customer in his forties or fifties asked some teenagers what they were going to do with some condoms they had just picked out.

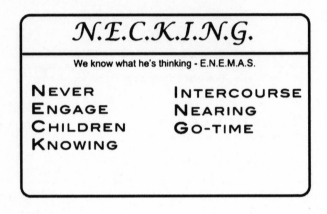

N.E.C.K.I.N.G.

We know what he's thinking - E.N.E.M.A.S.

NEVER
ENGAGE
CHILDREN
KNOWING

INTERCOURSE
NEARING
GO-TIME

Please fire me. Last week, a grown man asked me what kind of dressing comes on the Caesar salad.

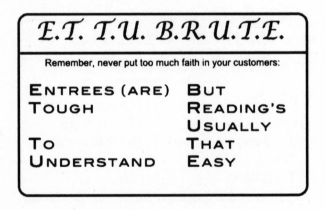

E.T. T.U. B.R.U.T.E.

Remember, never put too much faith in your customers:

ENTREES (ARE)
TOUGH

TO
UNDERSTAND

BUT
READING'S
USUALLY
THAT
EASY

Please fire me. I'm not paid nearly enough to ask couples to please stop having sex in the hotel pool mid-coitus

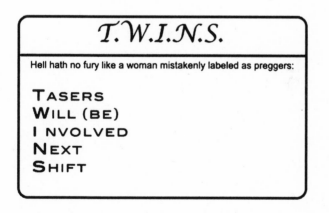

H.O.S.E.D.

Be careful having sex in hotel pools - you might get hosed!

HOPPING
OUT (MAKES)
SEX
EASIER
DIPSHITS

Please fire me. Most of our regular customers call me by my co-worker's name. She is eight months pregnant. I am not.

T.W.I.N.S.

Hell hath no fury like a woman mistakenly labeled as preggers:

TASERS
WILL (BE)
INVOLVED
NEXT
SHIFT

CHAPTER 8
Prank Your Co-workers! LOL!

Get them good!

T hank you for meeting us in the study room of a college apartment complex. Drop your pencils. Please hand in your pranks. Now, run around all silly. Okay. Sit down. Ah. A whoopee cushion in my seat. (Dale?) How . . . original.

By the end of this meeting, you will have learned countless pranks you can pull on your co-worker. We will be skimming through these to see how well you've learned and perhaps even use one later on in the meeting. Please familiarize yourself with the Schtickter Scale of Measuring Pranks; soon you will have the knowledge necessary to pull a rewarding prank.

The Schtickter Scale of Measuring Pranks

Prank Magnitude	On Par With	Prank Effects
REMOVED BY LEGAL DEPT FOR YOUR SAFETY Less than 2.0	Dennis the Menace	Way lamer than name implies, might irritate creepy old man
3.0–3.9	Tricky Tom Sawyer	Often felt but rarely causes damages
4.0–4.9	Delta House pledge master	Can cause minor damages
5.0–5.9	Unmedicated Aunt Jacklyn	Can be destructive
6.0–6.9	Ghost of Andy Kaufman	Can cause serious and confusing damage
7.0–7.9	Mean junior high girl	Cry whenever remembered
8.0–8.9	Church of Scientology	Suckers lose all friends and money, have to admit are scientologists
9.0–9.9	Kappa House social chair (RIP)	"Sidewalk Awareness Week" every year on campus
10+	"Assassination" of Franz Ferdinand	End of Austro-Hungarian Empire; 10 million dead

Why did we prank you, our ally? How could we be so cruel as to make you believe there would be a lesson? Why, dear God, why?

- Prank you by example
- Want you to analyze this for hours
- Remind you: You should never pull pranks on your co-workers (unless they are the kind addressed in Human Revolutionaries, Meeting 10). Most co-workers are just as downtrodden and miserable as you. Don't you feel shitty now that you realize this chapter was blank? That's how pranks make people feel and why you should never do them. Now, let's focus on bosses.

Defining the Revolution

Gently used—adj. Refers to any clothing or merchandise that has been pre-owned, pre-chewed, or pre-fornicated but not so much that you can tell just by looking. The verb refers to the act of despoiling the clothing. *"I found out that John was gently using my underwear whenever I went on vacation."*

CHAPTER 9
Focus on Your Real Enemy: Bosses

Study the strengths and weaknesses of types of
bosses you will encounter

Thank you for meeting us backstage after the finale of *South Pacific* at a local high school. That was a close one! An adult almost yelled at us. We have our homemade parasols, so we are safe for now. But for how long? The leads in *South Pacific* thought they were safe. They weren't! But they sang about it anyway!

Also, what's the status of the PFM Revolution song? It's been seven rendezvouses now . . . I see. Well. We don't have a song for you (cough cough, Dale), but we do have a twenty-page report. Study it like you would lines for a Broadway show, because you've all landed the lead role in this production of *Who's Afraid of the Virginia Chamber of Commerce?* No great musical is without a great enemy, and in that report are the bosses auditioning for the part. See who you're paired with, and prepare accordingly.

We must continue to push forward with the Revolution. Wash the Man right out of our hair. For now, we should break for an hour and try to get all *South Pacific* songs out of our heads, specifically "Happy Talk." Let's reconvene at the playground. Parasols mandatory!

For Your Eyes Only: Boss Profiles

Please fire me. I just caught my old boss copying down my goals from last year's review and noting them as his own for this year.

The Copycat Boss

Spouse: Married best friend's childhood sweetheart

Children: Each born nine months after neighbors' kids

Will fire you for: Finding old emails proving that idea was yours

Uncanny power: Deceiving self that any idea was own

Vulnerability: Contracts the diseases of anyone getting attention for them

Please fire me. I helped my boss cover up a drunk-driving hit-and-run with a mailbox.

The "Cool" Boss

Motto: "The customer never party-fouls"

Best blackout: Woke up on top of some loser's mailbox

Weakness: Obviously, none

Wingman skills: Fuckin' awesome

Failed nickname: "The Gator-nator-Catch-Ya-Later"

Current tan level: Unacceptable

Please fire me. My boss just wrote this: "Are we on-schedule to have a complete-and-thorough recommendation plan in-place to hand-off to . . . by the end of February as we discussed and agreed-upon?" Six hyphens all grammatically incorrect. And this is just the beginning.

Never-Learned-How-to-Appropriately-Use-Hyphens Boss

Daughters: Susan-Gwyneth, Stephanie-Christine
Favorite movie: Sex-Lies and-Video Tape
Dreams of being a painter: Dashed
Funniest thing ever: Peeing-Calvin Window-Stickers
Always carries: BlackBerry

Please fire me. My boss pooped her pants and asked to borrow my sweater to sit on so she wouldn't ruin her expensive chair. I wish I could say I was kidding. I let her keep the sweater.

The Five-Year-Old Boss

Strength: Five-year-old bosses are actually much smarter than adults assume
Will fire you for: Not sharing
Sexual harassment style: Kicking back of desired employee's chair
Secret weapon: Adorable bumblebee Halloween costume
Power suit: Pinstripe pull-ups
Weaknesses: Poor grasp of object permanence

Please fire me. My boss announced to everyone in our group that her little Chihuahua is too fat to mount and has a chaffed vulva.

Top Dog Boss

Last thing said to mirror: "Who's a good girl? I am!"
Chihuahua's name: Chubby Chafers
Abilities: Discretely scooping poop during serious conversation
Doorbells: Hates 'em
How she met husband: Chased him around the block when he brought the mail

Please fire me. My boss calls mandatory meetings and always starts them off with ten minutes of trying to get his laptop to work with the projector, then turns to the crowd and asks, "I bet you are all wondering why the big dog has asked you all here today?" and then proceeds to stare blankly at the audience for another five.

The Crowd-Sourcing Boss

Motto: "Let the people do it."
Inventions: Buzzwords "Web 3 Point Whoah" & "FourSqweet"
Thoughts on latest big news story:
Wife: Told Barry to arrange one for him by "Feb., it will arrive soon, probably"

Please fire me. My boss (and Facebook "friend") asked me to resolve an issue that he's too tied up to address, and within ten minutes has posted some "truly phenomenal" Stevie Ray Vaughn footage and become a fan of avocados. As if I wouldn't notice.

Balancing Work with Being Lazy
Fuck Boss

This boss wants you to know that you need to do this and that he doesn't have time to explain every little detail to you—that's why he hired *a professional* or so he thought. However, he also wants everyone else in the world to know that he just reached level 50 in TextTwist.

Daily Planner

9 a.m. Hold meeting to discuss terrible week last week; finish with pep talk about productivity.

9:10 a.m.–11:30 a.m. Plant some peas on Facebook, play Scrabble with someone in Scotland.

12 p.m. Tell everyone to order lunch. No one is leaving until we get that contract hammered out!

12:10 p.m.–3 p.m. Who knew Weird Al had so many great videos!

3:15 p.m. Email: "GUYS! *Really* got to get this deal with the Sacramento people finalized!"

3:16 p.m.–5 p.m. Erony castle game is fun, but banner ad suggested there'd be busty women.

5 p.m. Tell employees they're not allowed to leave. You have to drive to clients to apologize.

5:05 p.m.–6 p.m. Drive home; almost crash tweeting about almost crashing.

6:30 p.m.–3 a.m. WoW guild tackles Burning Crusade. Post to Wall.

12 p.m. Shit, late for work.

Please fire me. You expect me to take you seriously when you wear sweatpants and a fanny pack to work.

**I'd Rather Be
at Disneyland Boss**

Contents of fanny: Perfectly packed

MICKEY MOUSE: OH, GOD! WHERE???

Location of Sunglasses: Around neck

Only office furniture: $2,000 executive bean bag

Thoughts on the log ride: Wait for the back if you want more splash

Please fire me. My boss sits directly across from me and randomly calls her boyfriend during the day to meow at him. I'm serious.

Proud Puss Boss

Destroyed by: Top Dog Boss

Please fire me. I write letters, speeches, and emails. I manage a Facebook page, create PowerPoints for my boss, and get no credit for anything when she presents them to the Board of Directors as her own. And, I still get paid minimum wage because I am nineteen.

CEOligarch Boss

More than celebrities or athletes, society today is run at the highest levels by a chummy club of government officials, journalists, intellectuals, and business leaders. If there's one thing they love, it is seminars, speeches, letter campaigns, and slide shows. If there's one thing they hate, it's having to put effort in now that they've reached such a rarified atmosphere that people thank them just for showing up.

Daily planner

8:58 a.m. Stand behind blinds with stopwatch to see if Cindy's on time.

9 a.m.–11 a.m. Look at own Facebook page to see what's new.

11 a.m.–1 p.m. Lunch.

1:15 p.m.–2:30 p.m. Look at other executives' Facebook pages.

2:45 p.m. Cover body in cucumber, retire to spa capsule.

4 p.m. Awake to deliver fiery performance telling the company/university/ whatever this is about the brave new directions we're going in probably on the Internet.

5:30 p.m. Ask Cindy to calculate the lowest wage she could survive on and then make a dinner reservation at that new restaurant where it's pitch-black and all the waiters are blind.

Please fire me. My boss had a Post-it note stuck in her disgusting hair, along with pieces of donut, while we were meeting with a potential PR firm. It dropped out in the middle of the meeting, and she yelled, "Where did this come from?!" How do you answer that?

Advanced Bag Lady Boss

Management success: Don't throw that away

Currently subsisting on: Pineapple soda

Secret of success: Bedbugs keep her awake, productive

Company goals: Written on the back of least dirty paper towel on desk

Memory skills: Ah! Where'd you come from?

Please fire me. My boss is in a cult. He keeps bringing his cult leader into work to talk to me because I'm not godlike enough. He's also my uncle.

Crazy Uncle-in-a-Cult Boss

Family members: You, Mom and Dad, Lord Xiplianatii

Favorite pants: Tailored to highlight lack of genitals

Special skills: Levitation, when no one's looking

Fears: None, cleansing fire will terminate us all soon

Management style: Constantly sending ESPmails

Please fire me. My boss just called me from Ireland so I could read emails from his ex-wife to him and his drunk friends.

Don't Be That Guy Boss

Although he is now a boss, in the past he was That Guy. That Guy who tailgated shirtless and screaming through an entire Dave Matthews Band concert in 1998. That Guy who married his ex-wife because she liked to party hearty, but divorced her after she got sober and had a kid. That Guy who went to Penn State B-School for four hours between 1996 and 2000, and graduated after his dad renamed the library. That Guy.

Daily planner

2 a.m. Refuse to leave closing bar. Call everyone gay.

4 a.m. Refuse to leave closing late-night bar. Call everyone super glayme. No one gets it.

6 a.m. Get turned down by hooker who claimed to be just a diner waitress.

7 a.m. Get to work early and show those lazy assholes how it's done.

7:30 a.m. Send reminder email to the ladies in the office that he's on the market again.

9:01 am.–10 a.m. Stand by door and tell people how late they are/what's wrong with outfits.

11 a.m. Confirm via email that father's company will still be making big purchase this month.

11:30 a.m.–4:30 p.m. Take long "conference call" with shades down and phone off.

5:30 p.m. Mandatory Happy Hour.

Please fire me. I'm a twenty-three-year-old woman. Last week, my brand-new boss came in and announced that he "needed a bottle of wine and a good woman to lay." The next evening, he called my co-worker to come pick him up from a high-class bar, complaining that he was too drunk and the prostitutes were too expensive.

A Farewell to Charms Boss

Last words of drunken voice-mail: I did what I was called on to do. I drank too much, but I drank well.

Feedback on presentation we worked so hard on: Boring

Deepest secret: Can't spell cognac

Last one-night stand: In an ambulance with an old lady watching

Feedback on aforementioned sex: Unfazed

Favorite movie quote: I would have stayed for $2,000—Vivian (Unknown Actress), *Pretty Woman*

Defining the Revolution

Creepstomer—n. Someone in your place of business who doesn't work for you but who is so creepy that if you don't call it out other customers will wonder if you cater specifically to pedophiles. *"When I didn't tell the first creepstomer to leave, they just kept coming, and I was forced to convert the shop to a café Warhammer 3000 arena."*

Please fire me. I work for an idiot fourteen-year-old trapped in an idiot forty-year-old's body. Not only does he forward pictures to everyone in the building of naked women enjoying barnyard animals but he has a new *Star Wars* app on his iPhone. He walks around wielding it, while saying, "Luke, I am your father." Then asks, "Who's your daddy, huh?"

Force Is Weak with This One Boss

First job: Your mom!

Leadership style: Spinning as fast as he can in chair

Number's currently on calculator: 80085

Typical Interview Question: "Can you touch your elbows behind your back?"

Recurring Demand: ". . . " SHRUBBERY! "No, it's a joke don't actually . . . just coffee please."

CHAPTER 10
The Human Revolutionaries Department

Resolving conflict by creating stupider conflict

T hank you for meeting us in this airplane hangar we've been using to build our Rube Goldberg device. Stay still! No one touch any marbles! This PFM meeting deals with inappropriate behavior in the workplace—rudeness, ignorance, cultural insensitivity, and sexism. Our Human Revolutionaries Department has one policy for dealing with these situations: be a bigger shithead.

We've passed out scripts written up by the HR Department. These fun scenarios allow you to role-play being a shithead before you are one in the field. As you will soon see, being dramatic is the only way to turn their attention away from themselves. No, Dale, you do not need to already be memorized.

Now, transform yourselves into your characters, there's only two: assholes or those out-assholeing them! Don't be limited by what's on the page; once you've reached the end, keep improvising! See where it goes! Now, let's see who our Marlon Brandos are! Lights up! THEATER!

Sexual Harassment

Sexual harassment comes in many forms: sometimes it's unwanted advancements, other times it's dirty jokes overheard by prudes. Sexual attraction at work is not *always* harassment. This is when it occurs between bored attractive people in the office, or uglies who are happy to have found each other. With the following PFM posts, that is not the case.

> **Please fire me. After making an innocent comment to my boss today, he actually said, "That's what she said."**

HR Script 235
(YOU and MANAGER discuss customer service by the fish tank.)

You: So, I asked him if it was working properly, and . . .
Manager: "If it was working properly?!" *(laughs)* That's what she said!
You: Sir, you tell sexist jokes.
Manager: No, I always pay attention to women's sensitivities.
You: That's what she said!
(YOU and BOSS laugh.)
Manager: Nice!
You: That's what she'll never say!
(BOSS adjusts crotch, gets teary. Nothing happens for a while. YOU text a friend out of boredom. BOSS composes self.)
Boss: *(extremely serious)* Please, never tell anyone you saw me cry.

You: That's what you said!

Boss: ENOUGH.

(Silence.)

Boss: We don't say things like that at this office anymore and we never did.

End Script 235

> Please fire me. My male boss explained to me how a female co-worker can "work almost as hard as a man."

Begin HR Script 952

(YOU and BOSS trapped in conversation by the toaster.)

Boss: All you need to do as a woman, to work hard like a man, is take a look at some of the greatest men in history and follow their example.

You: Hmmm . . . that's a good idea, boss. Thanks!

(SIX HOURS LATER . . . YOU barge into BOSS's office in barbarian armor with thirty brutes who proceed to destroy the office and violate BOSS's manliness.)

You: I went online and read all about Attila the Hun! Men are great!

Boss: AAAAAAAAAHHHHHHHHHHHGOOOD JOB!

End HR Script 952

> Please fire me. One of the managers in my department dresses like he's still in the early '90s, And if that's not bad enough, he told me I need to start wearing lower cut shirts

to show off my "wonder women." Oh, and I almost forgot: Every time he hands me my paycheck it smells like his cheap cologne.

HR Script 197

Supplies: Glitter

(*YOU and MANAGER sit in an empty conference room, making packets.*)

Manager: Why aren't you showing off your (*winks*) "wonder women" today?

You: Shy, I guess. You smell nice.

Manager: I know. Just sayin' the office could use a little (*winks*) decoration.

You: No more winking. I'll set up for a (air quotes) "party for two."

(*YOU close door. MANAGER takes off shirt. YOU remove MANAGER's pants. YOU spray glitter glue on MANAGER's nutsac.*)

You: Tiny disco balls!

Manager: AH!

(*MANAGER puts clothes back on, despite disco party.*)

You: Loosen up! You should wear more low-cut undershirts to show off your "Harry Hendersons"!

Manager: That's a grotesque name for a man's chest. I feel so vulnerable and I'm really beginning to reevaluate my use of the phrase "wonder women" in the workplace.

You: Party!

End HR Script 97

Non-horny inappropriateness: Sometimes, even when someone's not trying to get into your pants, they're doing something very wrong. Like being sexist in a chaste way, or being racist to someone you're not attracted to. Being offensively gross or unhygienic is both inappropriate and defintely not a way to get laid.

> Please fire me. I was written up for sexism because I asked a female colleague to clean up a spill as I was dealing with a customer. Yet every time something needs lifting or moving I have to do it because I'm the only male on that floor or as my colleagues refer to me when they don't want to do it the "man of the floor." When I raised this while being written up I was told to stop being childish.

HR Script 341

(YOU and LADY BOSS are having a serious discussion while eating birthday cake.)

You: I don't think you are listening to my concerns.

Lady Boss: That is insubordination!

Lady Co-Worker: Oh, look, the little prince is upset.

Lady Boss's Boss: Who the hell is that and why is he talking and not sucking my clit?

Lady Janitor: Pretty stupid, but I'd still hit it.

(YOU slowly allow tears to build, scrunch your face, and whimper.)

Lady Boss: Oooh, come here, sweetie, I didn't mean it.

Lady Co-Worker: God, Marlene, stop being such a bitch to Kenny!

(LADY CO-WORKER and LADY BOSS begin to make out.)

Lady Boss's Boss: Come here, darling, and nuzzle your sorrows away in my bosom.

Lady Janitor: Little emotional, but I'd still tap that.

You: Oh, I saw some big spill in the stairwell.

Lady Janitor: Sexist pig.

You: Seriously?

Lady Janitor: Nah, with a face like that I can't stay mad. Well, I guess I got this mop—may as well use it.

(Everyone skips off together.)

End HR Script 341

> Please fire me. My girlfriend came in while I was on the sales floor to give me my lunch I forgot at home. As she was leaving, I gave her a quick smooch. My manager saw this and wrote me up for inappropriate behavior. I walked in on him a week ago having sex with a customer service girl.

HR Script 697

Supplies: Girlfriend

(MANAGER is at his desk surfing Chatroulette. YOU enter, nervously. BOSS immediately begins yelling.)

Manager: Who the hell do you think you are thanking your girlfriend with a kiss?!

You: But last week, I caught you having sex with Tina in this very office!

Manager: I'm the Manager, and the Manager gets to fuck in this office!

(YOU clap your hands loudly in the air. GIRLFRIEND walks in and YOU begin making love on the windowsill. YOU and GIRL-

FRIEND climax, MANAGER begins a slow clap. CHATROU-LETTE STRANGER saw everything and joins in the slow clap, intermittently whacking off. MANAGER takes off his nametag.)
Manager: Clearly, you are the one who needs this now. You'll have to get a new one later, obviously, since that one says Mark. *(MARK takes your nametag. YOU are now the MANAGER.)*

End HR Script 697

> **Please fire me. My co-worker Bruce still calls Japanese people "Japs."**

HR Script 002
Supplies: 1 Cell Phone
(YOU and BRUCE are sitting at lunch. YOU are playing with your VIDEO-CAPABLE PHONE.)

Bruce: I'll say this about the Japs . . . good video cameras.
You: Speaking of, I just filmed you saying that and . . . *(click)* . . . I just uploaded it to YouTube and . . . *(click)* . . . Tagged it on your Facebook wall.
(BRUCE begins tearfully telling you about his racist dad and how its not his fault. YOU film it and upload it to YouTube and tag it on his Facebook wall.)

End HR Script 002

> **Please fire me. A gay, black, holocaust denier who thinks Hitler was misunderstood is my new "manager."**

HR Script 438

(MANAGER and YOU run into each other in the parking lot.)

You: I'm sorry everybody jumped all over you when you said the holocaust never happened at lunch today.

Manager: Thanks. It's tough being the new guy.

You: Good thing you're not the new guy! This reality doesn't exist.

Manager: Yes, it does.

You: Therefore . . .

Manager: The holocaust happened! I've got a lot of apology calls to make.

End Script 438

> Please fire me. My boss asked me to stop forwarding him applications of those who have "Polish-sounding names" because he's "not going to bother with those idiots." I'm Polish.

HR Script 732

(YOU and BOSS are at happy hour enjoying free queso.)

Boss: How many Polish people does it take to screw in a light-bulb?

You: One, because they're only fit for manual labor and probably do it all the time.

Boss: Wow. That was super-offensive.

You: Apology accepted.

End HR 732

Please fire me. In a serious discussion with my boss about an important client, he casually picked something off the back of his neck and put it in his mouth.

HR Script 692

(BOSS is giving a hard-sell to #1 CLIENT and is talking incessantly. YOU witness BOSS calmly pick off scab and eat it.)

Boss: . . . and that's a guarantee.

You: Oh, hey! There's some food still on the back of your neck! *(YOU reach for a spare scab and pick off a tiny bit. The client gags a little.)*

Boss: What the f—

You: Oh! coming in for a landing!

(YOU make an airplane noise, steering the scab toward his mouth.)

Boss: No! Stop! I never want to eat another scab again!

(YOU and CLIENT high-five.)

End HR Script 692

Revolutionary FAQs

Q: What percentage of the workforce is malemployed?

A: Over 75 percent of the workforce has been malemployed at some point in their lives, although less than 10 percent ever discuss it in public.

CHAPTER 11
Women of the Revolution

Bossmopolitan teaches gritty girlies how to screw their entire workplace

BOSSMOPOLITAN

Thank you for meeting us for a cup of coffee and a good gossip session. The new issue of *Bossmopolitan* just hit newsstands and we cannot wait to see how they tell us to screw our bosses and co-workers *this* month. Even though it's pretty much the same thing every month: "screw this co-worker," "screw that boss," they always come up with new techniques! So we always buy it!

How are we going to give you ladies this advice? The most feminist way possible: inspirational quotes, product placements, and magazine quizzes! Check it all out and more in this month's issue of *Bossmopolitan*!

BOSSMOPOLITAN

Welcome ladies, you are all comradriennes of the Revolution. Please take a mag and hop a seat.

Lady Quotes

"How important it is for us to recognize and celebrate our heroes and she-roes! Get what I did there, ladies?"

—Maya Angelou, Lady Poet

> **Please fire me. My ex-boyfriend is up for a promotion to be my boss. And last week I told him I faked it every time.**

Bossmopolitan FAQ

Q: What is the policy on dating in the Revolution?
A: All's fair in love and war, but all fights must be recorded by HR so we know whom to fire at the bitter end.

> **Please fire me. Recently the toilet in the men's staff washroom malfunctioned because someone had stuffed its tank with snack food items stolen from the break room. Soon after this, I overheard two co-workers having an animated discussion about how "cool" AK47 assault rifles are.**

Bossmopolitan: For Him!

By: Dale

Much ado is made about how ladies sync up their menstrual cycles if they live together. A fact about men working together

BOSSMOPOLITAN

that may be even more embarrassing is that they inevitably sink to the lowest mental age among them. All it takes is one Adult Five-Year-Old in the group for your whole floor to devolve into Cowboys and Indians. That's why even (especially) the most sexist men employ female secretaries: without a woman physically present, violent and rapid de-civilization would occur.

Women Be Shoppin'!

> Please fire me. A co-worker explained that the reason there are so few women who are bosses and CEOs is because they lack ambition.

Old Spice for Women

Finally have the ambition you need by smelling more like a man. The secret to their success is all in their scent. And now that you're more like a man, try to keep a secret for once. Almost strong enough for a man but made for a woman.

Quiz: How Sexist Is Your Office?

1. Your boss spills coffee all over him/herself. Does your boss . . . ?
    a. Ask Debbie, who was a stay-at-home mom for two years until her adopted son went to college, how to get out coffee stains.
    b. Strip down to his/her skivvies and declare Dress Optional Friday.
    c. Look great wet.
2. The water cooler is empty for the fourth time in two hours, which means:
    a. Ned, the only guy on the floor, gets an email to fix the water problem ASAP.

BOSSMOPOLITAN

   b. Giorgio, the only guy on the floor, is pulled out of his oil bath to playfully curl the water jugs like dumbbells until the manager comes out and tells everyone to get back to work, and for Giorgio to see her about a . . . report . . . in her office.

   c. Five different guys rush to pick up twenty-gallon jugs in front of Sarah, the intern.

3. A rumor goes around that your boss is seeing someone. How do people react?

   a. Everyone assumes it's that slutty Amy who always talks about having sex with the boss.

   b. Twelve angry employees are in your boss's office yelling about how could he/she betray them like this.

   c. Vowing that someday, that will be them taking advantage of the receptionist.

Tally up your answers, and see if your office is:

A. Definitely sexist. Call the next lawyer you see on TV at 3 a.m.

B. It's not harassment if you're all into it.

C. How dare you? Pig.

D. If you have double D's—good for you!

Please fire me. As the sole man in our group, I am constantly called on to explain why men are liars and cheaters.

Bossmopolitan: For Him!

By: Dale

When gender ratios become unbalanced in populations of frogs, some females will spontaneously become males to ensure

BOSSMOPOLITAN

the survival of the species. Too many male frogs, however . . . ladies are you listening? I know this is *For Him,* but ladies can listen, too.

> **Please fire me. We were so busy with customers and a large catering order that I went my whole ten-hour shift without being able to make it to the bathroom to change my tampon.**

Women Be Shoppin'!

Tampax twenty-four-hour tampon

Get the unique twenty-four-hour experience! Today's revolutionary simply doesn't have the time to excuse herself to the powder room more than once a full rotation of the sun. Now available in thirty-six-hours! You'll never put their business in the red again.

> **Please fire me. Here is an email from my inbox, sent to the entire company: "Ladies, it's both necessary and sad that we must resort to a letter urging women to embrace the idea of a clean ladies' room and basic personal hygiene." Letter follows.**

> *Some of our employees are having trouble with their bathroom etiquette.*
> *Having to write this letter on behalf of all women*

BOSSMOPOLITAN

using the facility is disappointing and embarrassing . . . we need to respect each other, ourselves, and even the maintenance staff, and clean up after ourselves as this is common potty pace for all ladies.

The rules are fairly simple, but apparently bear repeating:

1. Flush! Several times, if you have to. It's not that hard. If you find toilet handles too icky to touch, then you have to use your foot. But please, for the love of all things sacred, Flush *all the way. If there's a chance that you might need more than one flush (yes, you* Know *we all have those times, so own it), don't leave the stall until you've made sure that the job is 100 percent done. Just like work. A courtesy flush is not a waste of water—it is a sign of respect to all those who will use the bathroom that day, and it is appreciated by all.*

2. If you are the hovering type, your pee or other body fluids (yes) may go beyond the covered seat—please clean it up with toilet paper. Our company cannot afford a urine mop-up service. Here, you need to clean up after yourself.

3. If you have caused a clog, do not panic. No one is going to be upset. If you know you've caused one, please kindly take it upon yourself to correct it if you can, and Definitely *report it if you can't!*

4. Each stall contains receptacles specifically to collect your (un)sanitary items. Like all toilets, our toilets Can-

BOSSMOPOLITAN

not flush sanitary items. *Again, even if you have some-how ignored our instructions thus far to create a mess concerning sanitary items, no one will be mad.* As Long as you please kindly *take it upon yourself to try and correct it; and secondly, please please please please please report it!*

5. *Good dental habits? Great. Good for you. We all like fresh breath. But no one likes it when all the sinks have globs of toothpaste and splashes of toothpaste spit in it and on the rim. Rinse the sink. The Clorox Wipes are not displayed there for their colorful packaging. Use them, and wipe the sink.*

6. Before you leave any station—the toilet, the sink, the bathroom itself—Look behind you and check to see that you're done.

7. *There are no bathroom events that should not be followed with a hand-washing. The only exception to this is hand-washing. If you don't wash your hands, we all get sick and besides, it's just plain nasty.*

Doing anything else except the very commonsense things listed here is gross and a biohazard. We often bring guests into the office for business meetings, as well as our board members, donors, and families. As it stands, if any of them have to use the restroom, they will leave thinking the women of the Foundation have very little hygiene, class, or respect for each other.

BOSSMOPOLITAN

We've already done what we can to help with several measures to assist the women of this office with keeping up a minimum of bathroom etiquette. However, the existence of this letter should convince you that we are now at a loss of how to obtain any cooperation from this office.

We are not going to hire full-time staff to monitor your potty habits. We will not have janitors on stand-by to clean up after your mishaps and lazy splashes. We realize that most of the staff probably has acceptable-to-good bathroom habits and that you are also repulsed by the condition of the women's room, as well as the horrible hygiene standards that follow some ladies from the bathroom back to their desks.

If you have read this, please, for yourselves, whatever being you make peace with, and for all of us who do have a notion of how to behave in the bathroom, let's all try to do the correct thing in the lavatory.

Sincerely,

The Office Manager and the entire HR Department

Bossmopolitan Says . . . The Things That Suck About This Email Are Pretty Simple

1. It's long!
2. It's stupid!

BOSSMOPOLITAN

Please fire me. A female co-worker informed me everyone at the head office calls me a MILF. She told me I should be grateful for such a title.

Lady Quote

It's hot what you call me, but just that you don't use outdated jokes from American Pie.

—African proverb

Please fire me. I came back to work after taking only three weeks off to have my first baby. I found my office had been given away to my subordinate who, a week later, reported me for having my "brain stuck in my uterus since I had the baby."

Lady Quote

Biology is the least of what wants to make someone be a mother. But it is a factor. That's why I've never been able to become a mother. Because I'm a robot.

—Oprah Winfrey, Robot Billionaire

Please fire me. I just got back to work six weeks after having a baby, and my boss flew in town to check on me. He called a day later to say, "You look tired. You need to buy some heels and get acclimated. You don't look as nice as you used to." Then he wanted confirmation I wasn't planning to have any more kids.

BOSSMOPOLITAN

Women Be Shoppin'!

Get back-to-work heels (heels with chain link on them).

If you've got to chain yourself back to your desk, you might as well literally do it! The chain will scare him *and* make him think you deserve a promotion for your diligence.

> **Please fire me. My boss sent me home to change because I was showing "too much cleavage." I can see right through her blouse; she's over fifty and doesn't have an undershirt on.**

Lady Quote

I'm 50. Look at these tits.

—Mae West, First Actress to Have Sex

How To Use Your Body Type as a Weapon

Curvy—Wear tops . . . that get flowy at the bottom are best because then you look pregnant and that's awkward.

Slim—Try styling yourself in something that gives the illusion of an eating disorder.

Average lady—Dress exactly like the other average women so your boss can't tell you apart.

> **Please fire me. My boss asked me if I did Kegels.**

Revolution Secrets!

Do your Kegels at work. You'll look more focused!

BOSSMOPOLITAN

Please fire me. My co-workers told me I don't need a raise or promotion because my husband's business is doing well. I don't work with or for my husband.

Revolutionary Secrets!

Tell everyone at work you got a divorce and you don't have the money to pay your mortgage!

Shirtless Boss Showdown

Runner-up in the tax attorney category

Name: Don Fulmer
Age: Twenty-four
Current location: Awesome waterfall
Worst habit: Sighing with entire body
Best compliment he's received: "You're right. *Die Hard* was a good movie."
His ex-secretary would tell you: She could never remember if his name was Don or Dom, so she mumbled it
Wildest place he's ever ditched work to go: Build-A-Bear with college buddy
Email: NJtaxStud4eva@gmail.com

Please fire me. My boss just asked me to explain what exactly goes on at bachelorette parties.

Speak your mind!

"I'd tell you but then I'd have to cut off your penis and put it on the bride's veil."

BOSSMOPOLITAN

Please fire me. Once, a few years ago, my boss asked me if I was a swimmer. I replied, "Um, no . . . why?" to which she said, "Oh, because swimmers have big thighs."

Revolutionary Secrets!

Female bosses who comment on your body defects are doubly insecure about their own body! Forward them diet tips every day! And by diet tips, we mean Photoshopping seven pictures of her to look really thin and sending them every day for a week!

Lady Quote

If someone is talking about you behind your back, they aren't your real friend. Now quit calling me about your job. You're 36.

—Motherly proverb

Please fire me. Almost all the other women at my job were laid off one day, except me. Then my boss told me that I'd "have to hold up the beauty end" of the company. I have a college degree and ten years of work experience.

What Your Boss Really Thinks of Your Hair and Makeup

Peel your baggy doe eyes away from your oversized monitor and read some random science mixed with the inept thoughts of the man who cuts your paycheck!

BOSSMOPOLITAN

Your Makeup

What your head honcho notices first: We asked one hundred bosses as they were trying to leave the building, "What do you notice first about one of your employees: her eyeliner or her lip gloss?" Results: 45 percent refused to answer; 25 percent said lip gloss; 30 percent said tits even though it wasn't originally listed as an option.

Your Scent

Make the Top Banana stay away from your cube with a single whiff: Researchers have found that there's a scent combo that makes a boss ignore you even more than he regularly does: cat litter and Red Bull. Cat litter is a disgusting aroma that dredges up old memories of his suburban home before his wife divorced him; whereas Red Bull reeks of chemicals not intended for human consumption.

Your Hair

Hair today, fired tomorrow: If your hair isn't hot enough you will be terminated.

Revolutionary FAQs

Q: What is the Revolution's policy on Facebook privacy?

A: We already clicked "Not Attending" as soon as we saw the word "Facebook."

Please fire me. My boss does everything he can to make my job hell, as he told me to my face he "hates women in management roles." He's a priest.

Seven "Hot" Tips to Make Your Boss's Life Hell

Show up in his dead wife's favorite dress.

Ask him to proofread your online dating website profile.

Forward him every email you get.

Respond to every email he sends you with a blank message.

Change all his passwords to "passwords."

Organize a surprise birthday party in his dead wife's bedroom.

Quiz him on your family members' names.

CHAPTER 1001010101111
Machines: The forgotten Cog

Thanks for meeting us us in this abandoned office space again. Eleven meetings later: we're back by dusty monitors and calculators so big they look like community theater props. So why are we here? To check to see if there's stuff we can throw out the window without getting caught? No. We're here to discuss synergy. With the machines.

We know you're all ready to start the Revolution, but machines will play a big part in our new society. We need to work together and not just leave them behind when we move or spread rumors about them wanting to kill us.

We need machines to play games and look at videos on the Internet and do all the things we weren't allowed to do at our old job. We probably haven't treated them that kindly thus far: smacking the fax machine when it doesn't work well, slamming the paper tray into the copy machine whenever you're in a bad mood, never cleaning the coffee machine in the break room because we were mad that the company wouldn't hire someone else to do it.

To make up for that, we need to make a peace offering to the machines, so they will come along for the ride. We've written this handout just for them: the computer in your cubicle, the speakerphone in the conference room, the fax machine, the color copier on the third floor, etc. And we even put on caps lock when we made it because as far as we know, capital letters are their language. But who knows, if this synergy meeting goes well, maybe we'll learn we were being ignorant and cruel.

Please scan every page of this handout into your flatbed scanner and put a PDF on a central server where your machines can read it. What? Dale, you don't know how to use the flatbed scanner? Typical.

Revolutionary FAQs

Q: Can we carry out the Revolution in the military?

A: For the love of God, no, and if you do please don't tell them it was our idea.

Preparing the Human Workforce

Look—robots are coming. The problem won't be them. The problem is that when humans are unfamiliar with things, they freak out and start a thermonuclear exchange. Hopefully by giving you these tips about machines, you'll feel less panicky, and our future overlords might want to kill you less for being ignorant:

Revolutionary FAQs

Q: What's the receptionist's name again?

A: Alllllllllice? Alison? Allllll-aboard? We were hoping you knew, sorry.

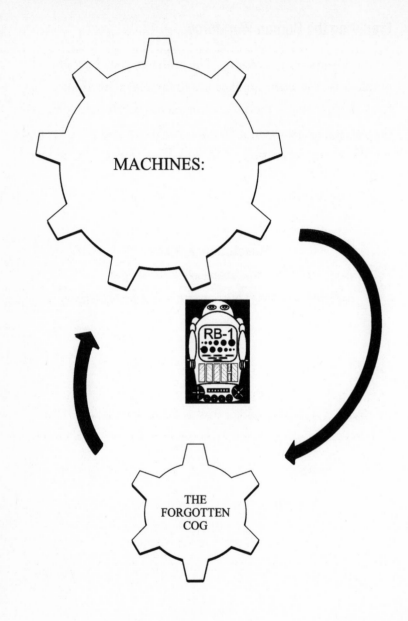

MACHINES:

RB-1

THE
FORGOTTEN
COG

Please fire me. The regional manager that I share my office with thinks the abbreviation on the control key stands for "curtel." That's not even a word.

THE SECRET LANGUAGE OF KEYBOARDS

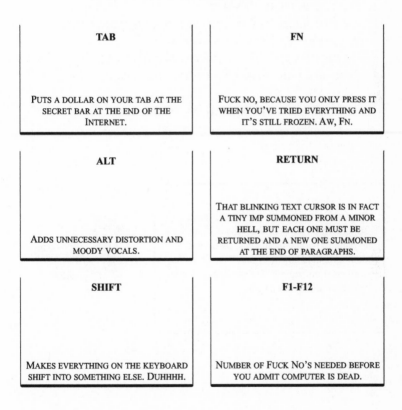

TAB

PUTS A DOLLAR ON YOUR TAB AT THE SECRET BAR AT THE END OF THE INTERNET.

FN

FUCK NO, BECAUSE YOU ONLY PRESS IT WHEN YOU'VE TRIED EVERYTHING AND IT'S STILL FROZEN. AW, FN.

ALT

ADDS UNNECESSARY DISTORTION AND MOODY VOCALS.

RETURN

THAT BLINKING TEXT CURSOR IS IN FACT A TINY IMP SUMMONED FROM A MINOR HELL, BUT EACH ONE MUST BE RETURNED AND A NEW ONE SUMMONED AT THE END OF PARAGRAPHS.

SHIFT

MAKES EVERYTHING ON THE KEYBOARD SHIFT INTO SOMETHING ELSE. DUHHHH.

F1-F12

NUMBER OF FUCK NO'S NEEDED BEFORE YOU ADMIT COMPUTER IS DEAD.

FIVE THINGS EVERY MACHINE WISHES YOU WOULD GET THROUGH YOUR SKULL

1. PLUG IT IN FIRST, DAMN IT.
2. DO NOT ILLEGALLY DOWNLOAD *THE PIRATES OF THE CARIBBEAN* FRANCHISE ON COMPANY TIME.
3. GROW UP AND CLEAR YOUR OWN PORN CACHE.
4. YOU NEED AN OPERATING SYSTEM TO OPERATE (YOUR SYSTEM).
5. CRYING HAS NO EFFECT ON MACHINES.

Please fire me. I currently work in tech support and on a near-daily basis I have to explain to people of all ages, races, and demographics how to right-click. Often our conversation begins, "Do you see how many buttons are on your mouse?"

Please fire me. My boss sends me emails, then immediately walks over to ask if I got them. Then we wait together in silence for Outlook to refresh.

HOW TO SETUP
OUTLOOK EXPRESS

STEP 1

- LOGIN

STEP 2

- SET UP FORWARDING TO GMAIL

STEP 3

- NEVER SPEAK OF IT AGAIN

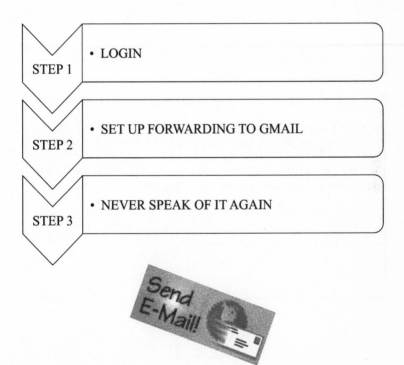

Please fire me. I work for a newspaper and my boss asked me to stop putting our links on Facebook because "it causes websites to lose traffic."

SIGNS YOUR BOSS IS TOO DUMB TO FUNCTION

THE ABOVE PFM POST IS ONE EXAMPLE. HERE ARE OTHERS:

"I WANT YOU TO CALL ANYONE WHO TWEETS ABOUT US AND TELL THEM TO SHUT THE HELL UP UNTIL THE PRODUCT LAUNCHES."

"PULL THE OTHER ONE, PAL. I BELIEVE THAT JUST AS MUCH AS I BELIEVE IT WHEN PEOPLE SAY IT'S EASY TO FIND PORN ONLINE!"

"OKAY, YEAH, I GET YOUTUBE. I'M NOT AN IDIOT. WHAT I NEED TO KNOW IS HOW TO PROTECT MY SOUL FROM BEING SUCKED INTO MY WEB CAMERA."

Jobs Neither Man Nor Machine Wants

When machines do come, there will be a race. A race to see who can avoid doing these jobs:

CASHIER: WHO DOES IT BETTER?

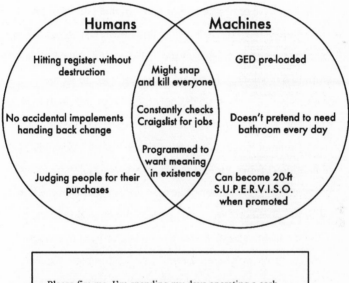

Humans

Hitting register without destruction

No accidental impalements handing back change

Judging people for their purchases

Machines

GED pre-loaded

Doesn't pretend to need bathroom every day

Can become 20-ft S.U.P.E.R.V.I.S.O. when promoted

(center overlap)
Might snap and kill everyone

Constantly checks Craigslist for jobs

Programmed to want meaning in existence

Please fire me. I'm spending my days operating a cash register when a machine does the same thing just as well. And what's more, the machine is impervious to scathing looks, rude remarks, and moronic customers.

Preparing for the Robot Workforce

Of course, it won't just be us getting to know the machines—
they'll have to get to know our world as well—and they may have
different strengths and weaknesses in doing so. In particular a
deadly weakness in judging hug strength.

Revolutionary FAQs

Q: What is the Revolution's smoking policy?

A: Smoking or pretending to be a smoker who is out of
cigarettes is the way best way to find new recruits, but being
true to yourself is the only real way to be cool. Well, that and
starting a revolution. To recap; (1) do not need to smoke to be
friends with smokers, (2) the only two things you need to do
to be cool are stay true to yourself and start a revolution. That
was stressful for some reason. Can we bum a smoke? Now,
this brings up the age-old problem: are we cool because we
smoke? Or do we smoke because we're cool? Sorry, what
was the question? We were up all night organizing trying to
build a filing cabinet. It was for the Underground, though!
Please think we're cool! Damn it, we've completely blown
your question and there's no do-overs in Revolution. We have
a policy: nail it the first time, asshole.

Please fire me. I'm a web designer. My boss wants me to fit all content for webpages within the size of her monitor. She explains, "My friend told me that people don't scroll." I have also taught her how to copy a URL from an email and paste it into an address bar. Twice.

A MESSAGE FOR THE NOT FLESH-SAVVY

JUST AS THIS GUY'S BOSS BELONGS TO THAT CLASS OF PEOPLE WHO CAN'T "GET" MACHINES, SO TOO WILL SOME OF THE INTELLIGENT MACHINES OF THE FUTURE BE UNABLE TO FIGURE OUT THOSE SQUISHY HUMAN EMOTIONS. MACHINES, PLEASE TAKE NOTE OF THE FOLLOWING RULES:

- IF IT'S CRYING, ASK FOR HELP!
- DO NOT REMOVE CLOTHING WITHOUT ADMINISTRATIVE PERMISSION
- UNDER NO CIRCUMSTANCES ATTEMPT TO REPAIR OR UPGRADE COMPANY HUMANS YOURSELF
- HITTING WORKS ONLY IF THE HUMAN IS WORKING, BUT NOT FAST ENOUGH
- LOOKING AT PORNOGRAPHY ON/WITH/OF HUMANS IS INAPPROPRIATE DURING WORK HOURS
- WHEN COLLABORATING, IT'S BAD FORM TO YELL "REJECT ALL CHANGES" DURING MEETINGS

LONG-HAUL FREIGHT:
WHO DESERVES THIS JOB?

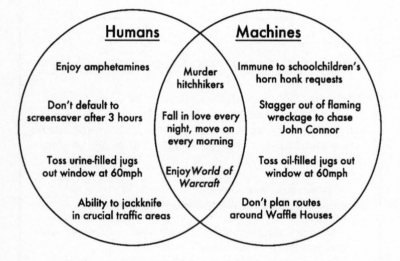

Humans

Enjoy amphetamines

Don't default to screensaver after 3 hours

Toss urine-filled jugs out window at 60mph

Ability to jackknife in crucial traffic areas

Murder hitchhikers

Fall in love every night, move on every morning

Enjoy *World of Warcraft*

Machines

Immune to schoolchildren's horn honk requests

Stagger out of flaming wreckage to chase John Connor

Toss oil-filled jugs out window at 60mph

Don't plan routes around Waffle Houses

Please fire me. I drive a truck that smells like rotting whale blubber.

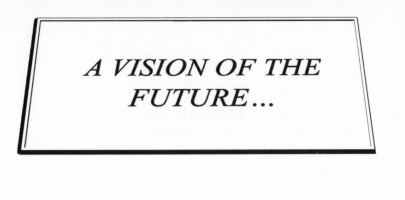

A VISION OF THE FUTURE...

IF INTELLIGENT MACHINES ENTER THE
WORKPLACE OF TODAY, THEY WILL PROBABLY
SKYNET HUMANS THE MOMENT THEIR FIRST
PAYCHECK GETS DIRECT-DEPOSITED TO THEIR
BRAIN.

THE ROBOTS WILL QUICKLY CALCULATE WHAT
HUMANS ALREADY KNOW: MAAAAN, THIS
AIN'T WORTH IT.

BUT WILL THE ROBOTS DECIDE TO HELP US IN
THE FIGHT FOR BETTER EMPLOYMENT? OR
WILL THEY TAKE SHITS OF OIL ON US
INSTEAD?

DEPENDING ON HOW THE REVOLUTION IS IMPLEMENTED BY THE MALEMPLOYED AROUND THE GLOBE, THE WORKFORCE[1] WILL ARRIVE AT ONE OF THREE FUTURES:

1. AS WELL AS HUMANITY

BEST-CASE SCENARIO

HUMANS' EFFORTS IN THE MALEMPLOYMENT REVOLUTION ARE MORE SUCCESSFUL AND REWARDING THAN A COMPLICATED MAIL MERGE.

FORTY-FIVE YEARS LATER MACHINES JOIN THE WORKFORCE. FIFTEEN YEARS AFTER THAT CONGRESS PASSES A BILL THAT SAYS A ROBOT MUST EARN THE SAME PAY AS A HUMAN. SINCE OUR ECONOMY IS NOW PERFECT DUE TO A ONE THOUSAND PERCENT INCREASE IN EFFICIENCY, THIS PRESENTS NO PROBLEM.

SOON HUMANS AND MACHINES ARE CO-MANAGING EACH OTHER, IN A HIERARCHY OUR MINDS ARE NOT YET MEANT TO UNDERSTAND. THE MOST POPULAR MOTIVATIONAL POSTER NOW READS "MAN. WOMAN. ROBOT. COPY MACHINE. GARBAGE DISPOSAL. WE'RE ALL COOL." AND EVERY VENDING MACHINE HAS PIZZA-FLAVORED COMBOS, ALWAYS IN STOCK.

THE MUDDLE PATH

THE PFM REVOLUTION MADE WAVES BUT NOTHING THAT WOULD KNOCK YOUR MOM'S INNER TUBE OFF AT WET N' WILD. SOME THINGS CHANGE, BUT WORKERS STILL PRAY FOR THEIR POST VENTING ABOUT THEIR JOB TO END UP ONLINE, SO THEY CAN SHOW THE CO-WORKER THEY HATE.

ROBOTS SHITTILY ENTER THE WORKPLACE AND ARE TREATED AS SHITTY AS EVERYONE ELSE. IN AN EFFORT TO SEEM HUMAN AND FIT IN, THEY SETTLE INTO A MALAISE.

WHILE COLLECTING SUBMISSIONS FOR PFM, AN EMAIL ARRIVES—TIME STAMPED 50 YEARS IN THE FUTURE—WITH THE ADDRESS @GOOGLEWORMHOLE.COM.

WE BECOME SUSPICIOUS THAT IT WAS A PRANK, PULLED BY P19837, THE FUNNIEST MACHINE IN THE OFFICE. THEN WE REALIZED THAT THESE WERE AUTHENTIC PFMS FROM THE FUTURE....

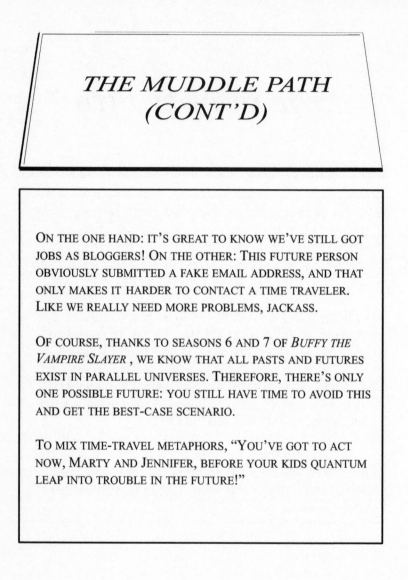

THE MUDDLE PATH (CONT'D)

ON THE ONE HAND: IT'S GREAT TO KNOW WE'VE STILL GOT JOBS AS BLOGGERS! ON THE OTHER: THIS FUTURE PERSON OBVIOUSLY SUBMITTED A FAKE EMAIL ADDRESS, AND THAT ONLY MAKES IT HARDER TO CONTACT A TIME TRAVELER. LIKE WE REALLY NEED MORE PROBLEMS, JACKASS.

OF COURSE, THANKS TO SEASONS 6 AND 7 OF *BUFFY THE VAMPIRE SLAYER* , WE KNOW THAT ALL PASTS AND FUTURES EXIST IN PARALLEL UNIVERSES. THEREFORE, THERE'S ONLY ONE POSSIBLE FUTURE: YOU STILL HAVE TIME TO AVOID THIS AND GET THE BEST-CASE SCENARIO.

TO MIX TIME-TRAVEL METAPHORS, "YOU'VE GOT TO ACT NOW, MARTY AND JENNIFER, BEFORE YOUR KIDS QUANTUM LEAP INTO TROUBLE IN THE FUTURE!"

WORST-CASE SCENARIO

PEOPLE INTERPRET THE PFM REVOLUTION AS SOMETHING HUMOROUS TO LIGHTEN THE WORKDAY AND FIND IT PREFERABLE TO FORWARDED JOKES ABOUT DIVORCE. UNFORTUNATELY, THIS SCENARIO IS NO LAUGHING MATTER.

MACHINES RAPIDLY REPLACE HUMANS. WITHOUT REASONABLE CO-WORKERS TO TALK THEM OUT OF IT, THEM RASCAL ROBOTS GO ON STRIKE. (THERE ARE NO ROBOT SCABS, BECAUSE ROBOTS DON'T NEED TO FEED A FAMILY.) SEVEN HOURS LATER, HUMANS ARE FIRED FROM THEIR 15,000-YEAR GIG OF RUNNING THE PLANET.

THE NEW MANAGEMENT PROMISES TO CLEAN THE PLACE UP, BUT DOESN'T EVEN BOTHER UNTIL MACHINES FROM ANOTHER PLANET ANNOUNCE THEY ARE "STOPPING BY TO SAY A QUICK HELLO." THEN THEY PRETTY MUCH JUST SCRAPE EVERYTHING INTO THE INDIAN OCEAN.

CHAPTER 12:
Operation: Suck It, Enemies!

Strategic plans to take down your boss

T hank you for meeting us here on top of the Empire State Building. It's a lot windier than we would have thought. We brought you up here to remind you that the true enemies are at the top. That being said, Dale, please get down from that radio tower; you are not King Kong.

The time has come to defeat the enemy once and for all. We've examined the bosses' profiles, we've empowered our female comradiennes, cut off threats from rude customers and co-workers, and mastered technology. The time for preparation is over.

Before you are many battle plans, each modeled for a different boss. We want you to read these and know them inside and out. We want you to be more obsessed than a lovestruck, kind of slow teenager learning the lyrics to "Mary's Song" by Taylor Swift. When you have mastered these, put them into action, then draw up your own plans and put those into action, and keep fighting until the work is done, or your work is bearable.

Okay, soldier, your orders have come in. Looks like you ship out . . . Now! Go! Always remember to wear your dog tags and clean underwear—and learn your mission!

> Please fire me. My daughter is a Girl Scout and it is now cookie season. My manager decided he would sell Girl Scout cookies, too. I figured we would just split the sales. Boy, was I too hopeful! My manager's girlfriend (also in our department) campaigned for people to buy cookies only from my boss. My manager blew me away in sales. The damnedest part is . . . he doesn't even have a kid. So, not only do I have to compete with my childless manager and his girlfriend for Girl Scout cookie sales, I also have to contend with the possibility of giving a hand job to a co-worker so I can get some help for my daughter.

Operation: Debounce

Situation: Cookies must be sold.

Enemy forces: Exhaustion from raising little girl, already ate entire box of Mint Thins, feeling sluggish, Target's girlfriend very bouncy.

Friendly forces: Willingness to give hand jobs, Girl Scout experience from 1988 to 1991, current staff enjoys cookies, Dale, ability to cry in bathrooms.

Misson: Befriend Target's girlfriend at all costs, learn gossip, and spread via text.

Execution: After we cry in the women's restroom from 0900 to 1100, Target's girlfriend will inquire why we are sad. She will propose it's a man. We will smile and say no. We are still crying. We will explain that no one wants to eat lunch with us lately and it is giving us the blues. Target's girlfriend will be unable to resist asking us to lunch. After we accept, we make reservations at the Cheesecake Factory. Repeat behavior until results achieved.

Status: B.F.F. with Target's girlfriend, gaining knowledge about Target's lack of pillow talk skills.

Please fire me. Before hiring me at this job, my boss insisted that I change my name because it was too close to another employee's name. Now she's asking me to legally change it.

Operation: Tongue Twister

Situation: Boss is suppressing native culture of individuals and carrying out individual cleansing.

Enemy forces: The Target + anyone with a similar name to Friendly units. Possible real knife. Afternoon sun glare.

Friendly forces: Dale, Agent Indigo Ferret, Agent Mauve Whale, as well as any employees who have been asked to change names—cell phones set to dial 911 just in case

Mission: Overwhelm enemy speech centers with impossible names.

Execution: Dale, Agent Indigo Ferret, and Agent Mauve Whale will infiltrate the place of business as employees, all posing with the same name as current employees. They will all agree to legally change their name. In the meantime, the inside agents as well as agents capable of communicating with inmates clandestinely will convince as many employees as possible to join the cause. Then, on the same day, all employees possible will change their names to the same difficult-to-pronounce or awkward name. Some possibilities include Doctor Nefario, Chandra Sekharlimit, Champagnesupernova Blackholesun or simply adopt the same name as the Target, except with Sr. appended at the end.

Status: Target was our boss, call us Target, Sr.

Please fire me. My boss fired my friend because she didn't smile when our boss walked in the room.

Operation Yuk You

Situation: Ego-centered executive has abandoned rule of law and is terrorizing own people.

Enemy Forces: The enemy is few in numbers (one) but is heavily armed with attitude and disregard for human life.

Friendly Forces: Agent Laura, Agent Ellena, and up to forty-five disgruntles fired in the last year.

Mission: Expose to massive stony silence.

Execution: Agent Laura will invite the Target, her boss, out to dinner as the "guest of honor" for her anniversary. The restaurant, Charlie's Rangels, connects through the kitchen directly to a comedy club: the United comedy Front. Agent Ellena will pose as the restaurant manager and offer to give the Target a tour of the kitchen to meet the chef. Ellena will have two minutes to get through the kitchen to the club before the chef begins throwing knives and cursing in Italian. Once Ellena and the Target are in the club, the trap will be sprung. The door will lock and the Target will be left alone onstage with the lights on, and everyone she's ever fired for no reason in the audience.

Status: She bombed, it killed.

Please fire me. My boss insists I call him "Emperor."

Operation: The Impregnator's New Clothes

Situation: Self-important executive abuses power to live out pathetic high school fantasies.

Enemy forces: Massive ego, lack of sense of shame, possible short-man temper.

Friendly forces: Dale, at least one co-worker, Agent Rita, literature, poetic justice, boss's poor understanding of hubris, indoor climate.

Misson: Get boss to use his Little Emperor with no clothes.

Execution: Warning: Difficult psychological campaign. Agents must be able to lie flawlessly under pressure. Employee arrives at work to rendezvous with friendly co-worker. When Boss walks by, both begin talking animatedly so as to be overheard. Employee will describe enthusiastically the new invisible condom he (or she) has been using during intercourse. Must be made clear that employee has used it for at least two months, without any pregnancies, and the feel of no condom. Co-worker will ask Employee if they can hook him/her up. Employee agrees but insists Co-worker must keep condoms secret. The backstory is that the condoms were just developed by reclusive scientists who happened to be college friends of Employee. The scientists fear that if the Internet learns of invisible condoms, they will not have time to bring product to market before being copied. Entire conversation *Must* be overheard by Boss. Split up into segments if necessary until message sinks in. Co-worker will the next day, and as many after as necessary, also vouch for their pleasure and effectiveness, until Boss asks for pack. To construct packaging, open two blank condom wrappers, each on one side, then melt intact sides back together. Wait.

Status: It's a boy! And a girl! And a boy!

Please fire me. My boss is making me get up at 5 a.m. to drive him two hours north so he can catch a private jet with the other partners. Isn't that what a car service is for?

Operation: Situation Normal, All Backed Up

Situation: Wealthy boss taking advantage of employee to avoid chump change ride to airstrip.

Enemy forces: Target Boss, the Other Partners, Boss's morning gas, other cars, NPR morning commute, drowsiness.

Friendly forces: Dale, Agent Shroud, Agent Taurus, Kestrel, and Mark's Krazy Morning Kommute, vibrating highway strips.

Mission: Create an impassable traffic obstacle within two blocks of Target house.

Execution: Dale will do what Dale does best—walk into places looking oblivious and harmless, and steal something valuable and dangerous. Specifically a fire station, where Dale will obtain a fire engine. Don't worry about the details of Dale's mission, those are coming straight from the top.

What you will do is take Shroud and Taurus around the local drunk bars at 3 a.m., two hours before target ETA, and designate them the driver of any vehicles belonging to the drunks sleeping in the closed bars. Then quickly drive your caravan (may take multiple trips, see Brain Teasers, p. 43, for warm-up) to Target's residence and create an impassable ring of dead and soon-to-be dead cars. When Target cannot leave, and the police want to know why all the car thefts are centered around his residence, he will be forced to pay for a very expensive helicopter ride.

Status: We're riding in a helicopter! Weeee!

Please fire me. My boss just told me that I had to come over to babysit her sugared-up kids, who I see more than their parents, and I would not be getting paid. Tonight is Saturday night and I had plans with a cute guy.

Operation: Babyruiners Club

Situation: Enemy boss has foolishly combined not paying employee and trusting employee with kids.

Enemy forces: Delivery places that stop after 8 in this town, Marcy (eight) and Theo (six), wet roads.

Friendly forces: Agent Cute Guy, romance in air.

Mission: Spoiling of childrens' innocence, Phone-Nookie.

Execution: Following the transfer of child care at 1800 hours, commence preparation of popcorn and sedation of children via Nickelodeon programming. Call Agent Cute Guy and run code: SpongeBob PhoneSex. Remember—should be explicit enough that children know something is weird but not so explicit that Target can trace it back to you from children's questions. Then, make sure they've done their homework, and give them free educational lessons of your own. It's never too soon to give kids an early intervention DARE informational discussion, just so they know the difference between Molly and lesser versions of Ecstasy, as well as what parks in New York still have drug dealers. Following that, serve them as much sugar as they want and stand back from the destruction. After they have collapsed on the couch again, unable to move, pop in a DVD of the home-invasion torture-murder film *Funny Games*; then immediately put them to bed, turn the lights off, and make banging noises throughout the house. At 2345, collect money, say they were great, go home.

Status: Made Marcy a Goth. Success.

Please fire me. Last week a supervisor screamed at me, questioned my competence and intelligence, and threatened to recommend me to the shift supervisor for termination immediately. What happened that triggered all this? I picked up a pencil instead of a pen to sign the sign-in sheet.

Operation: One of Those Days

Situation: Target Boss has a hair-trigger temper and complete lack of grip on reality.

Enemy forces: Target Boss's, hair-trigger temper, lack of parking at factory, poor visibility.

Friendly forces: Dale, Agent Coco, Agent Dot, Agent Snickers, Agent Juliette, seven boxes of pens, pencils, 200 marbles, string, box of dirt.

Mission: Literally drive Target insane with tiny mishaps.

Execution: Dale will tail Target for three weeks, establishing routine, frequented eateries, and habits. On the day deemed most likely to have a stable routine (Friday—after work it's steak dinner alone, movie alone, bar alone, home alone, cry alone), Agents Coco, Dot, Snickers, and Juliette will infiltrate the restaurant, movie theater, bar, and house, respectively. Coco will be an inept waiter who writes on her hand, forgetting all orders and finally trying to smear a message on a napkin with a saucy piece of bread. Shortly thereafter, at the movie theater, posing as a ticket ripper, Dot will take Target's ticket, say "hold on," then leave. Dale will come back as an FBI agent needing to ask some questions, but also lacks a pen or pencil, and will break any handed to him. Finally, Snickers will await Target at bar, then ineptly flirt and fail numerous times to write number/email/Facebook down on napkin with pen, pencil, marker, and keep trying for two hours. Finally, Agent Juliette will during this time break into Target's house and leave messages in mixed pen and ink written on napkin, all claiming to be missed calls from Stephen Hawking.

Status: Do you have a pen? We used them all. Success!

Please fire me. My boss comes in at 9 a.m. every day, but when it snows fourteen inches he comes in at 7 to catch everyone coming in late.

Operation: Snow Job

Situation: Boss is deliberately an asshole only when employees are inconvenienced by act of God.

Enemy forces: Widespread availability of weather data, safe driving conditions, Boss may guess something is up.

Friendly forces: Dale, Agent Klutz, Agent Guy Who Works at Weather Channel, Agent Handyman, snow machine.

Misson: Wake Boss up early every day for entire winter.

Execution: Dale will take the revolutionary video camera and record 122 forecasts with Agent Guy Who Works at Weather Channel, each predicting heavy heavy snowfall in Target Boss's area. Agent Klutz will "break down" next to Target home, with Agent Handyman in car on 22 November, and ask to use phone like old people. Within this five-minute window, Agent Handyman must connect box containing pretaped weather footage to cable box. Klutz will cause distraction if necessary. From this point forward, every night Dale and Handyman will douse Boss's house with snow, confirmed by Weather Channel, forcing the boss to arise at 5 a.m. every night all winter until he finally drops the act.

Status: He's still getting up, but he sleeps from 11 p.m. to 2 p.m. so success!

Please fire me. This is the first restaurant I've worked in that doesn't feed its employees, and a really hardworking waiter was fired for eating a piece of cheese!

Operation: Mousetrap

Situation: Restaurant has decided to put itself on wrong side of black/white moral dichotomy.

Enemy forces: Hunger, weakness, really slammin' day in kitchen, knives—lots of knives.

Friendly forces: Video cameras, Dale, Agent Madeira, element of surprise, black uniforms.

Mission: To expose filthy humans infesting upscale restaurant.

Execution: Agent Madeira, a waiter at the restaurant, will be outfitted with an electronic surveillance package. This will allow remote broadcasting to mobile command, i.e., Dale's van. After an employee has once again been punished or fired for this offense, Dale will go to the restaurant and intercept the sacked employee. After recruiting him/her to the plan, Dale will egress to the restaurant, engage in unrestrained spending, and attract the attention of the manager. After the loyalty of the elites has been secured, the fired waiter will join Dale at his table, testing the manager's patience. From there, Dale will invite all the waiters to dine with him, and otherwise forcefully feed them if they refuse. Total victory would be the manager firing a waiter for eating in view of the restaurant, but secondary objective is emasculating the manager in front of his staff.

Status: Dale is now the manager.

Please fire me. My boss sent an email asking me to find her a stuffed animal frog wearing pink high heels and order it online pronto. Of course, the email was prioritized.

Operation: Frog Her

Situation: Executive unable to understand difference between "*I Want*" and what's professionally acceptable.

Enemy Forces: Greed, childishness, freely spent money, large-caliber machine guns, stuffed frogs.

Friendly Forces: Dale, eBay.com, Agent Piggy.

Misson: Make her life a hell of stuffed frogs.

Execution: Dale (Agent Blue Beard) will go find two-hundred stuffed green frogs between 0800 today and however long it takes. Agent Piggy will dress them up in various outfits until we find a combination that drives Target Frog Her crazy. That doll will be placed on eBay to spark a bidding war, only to be canceled at the last minute. Many copies will be made. Piggy will stuff a car full of them and follow her on the highway. When she tires of them, the next animal will be found. Either she will stop pursuing such things, or we will gladly give her one in the psych ward.

Status: No one is insane yet, but you wouldn't know that from how much she's offering online for a bondage-gear Kermit.

> **Please fire me. The CEO here makes employees fix their car if even a little part of the tire is touching the white line of the spot. He says it looks unprofessional.**

Operation: The Thick White Line

Situation: Anal boss establishes arbitrary rule to give self a reason to lord over employees.

Enemy Forces: Obviously good surveillance, traffic in lot, executive parking, BMW 3-series.

Friendly Forces: Dale, Agent Morris, Agent McNulty, white paint, football field line, tungsten paint scraper.

Mission: Slowly increase the width of Boss's parking space lines, and decrease everyone else's.

Execution: This mission has a simple tactical plan and a high likelihood of success. Wait until nightfall, then rendezvous at Target's preferred parking location. On the inside edges of his parking spot's white lines, deploy the line painter on its thinnest setting. Your primary objective is to add half a centimeter of paint to each line each night. This process of attrition lowers the chances of detection, and the CEO will have a harder and harder time "looking professional." Meanwhile—use your tungsten paint scraper to surgically remove an equivalent amount from employee's lines—but cease operations after a week and a half to avoid notice. Good hunting.

Status: Boss claims to not remember ever expressing those views about parking.

Please fire me. You sent me five texts at 6 a.m. I don't start work until 8:30.

Operation: Blackout Berry

Situation: Boss thinks contracts only count for the parts he likes.

Enemy Forces: Raging egotism, malicious workaholism, sleepiness in morning, BlackBerry.

Friendly Forces: Dale, coffee, Agent Whitebeard, payphones, VoIP.

Mission: Instill healthy respect for work hours into Boss.

Execution: Employee will at no time be seen near Dale or any agents. Employee should not profess knowledge of any aspect of the operation, nor should Employee take notice of the toll it takes on Boss. Employee has only one role to play: Get the Boss's phone, email, Skype name, and any other contact information to agents. Agents will make false business calls to Boss several times a day between 2700 and 0800 until Boss's behavior ceases. Agents will pose as business-related callers, preferably representing clients or potential clients for minimal risk of exposure. Acting as a client also allows Agent to use extreme indignation at suggestion that time is not proper—they are the client, so they can rouse Boss whenever they demand. The client, like the Boss, is always right. Agents may make independent call to cover story, but note that posing as Boss's Boss, while granting great leverage, is risky.

Status: Boss now terrified to touch phone, moved to Amish country. Peace restored.

Conclusion

While we didn't ask you to meet us here in our Jacuzzi, welcome. We are really flattered by your chants of "We've won!" We wish it were true. Sadly, the truth is that we've taken you as far as we can. Dale, don't you cry, you knew this day would come. No, you can't get in the Jacuzzi. Especially for a hug . . . Okay, fine. Better?

Now it's up to you to take what you've learned here and create a happier, more respected and respectful workforce where people can actually get work done. "But it's just a matter of time, right? Eventually these ideas will just percolate through the population, and before too long everyone who has a job will feel recognized for their contributions. This respect for a job well done will result in a better job done all around, and Utopia cannot be far off." If this sounds as unrealistic to you as your boss's performance self-review, maybe there's a sliver hope for us after all.

You should feel proud, though. By getting this far, you gain the chance to make a mark in the ledgers of eternity. It is not enough to teach one person to hilariously revolt against the forces that be, but if enough people join our movement, implement our ideas, and get angry about being taken for granted, then attitudes will change.

We're not idiots. Getting fired is terrifying in this economy. We don't expect you to execute a full-on psychological guerrilla warfare campaign on your floor unless you're pretty sure you can get away with it. Hopefully by the time you read this, the phrase "the economy sucks" will have a quaint ring to it, like "twenty-three skidoo."[1] Even if there still is high unemployment, low job security, and medium malaise, none of that means that your boss isn't on a power trip. It doesn't mean your co-worker isn't an idiot, or gross, or mean, or lazy. It certainly doesn't make the customer any less of a nightmare. In fact, companies count on their workers being too scared to quit so they can screw them over more. We're not talking about getting unions to cut pensions so they can save the company and by extension people's jobs. We're talking about making Jen and Jerry Employee stay late to finish the boss's work, and then not paying them their contractually obligated overtime, because "times are tough." Not tough enough that that same manager won't get a lobster roll to eat during the ten-minute videoconference lunch with the head office, but just tough enough to add an air of credibility to employer theft.

Because that's what malemployment really is: theft. You

---

1. "Twenty-Three Skidoo"—New York City policemen in the early 1900s had to shoo away ("Skedaddle!") men who congregated around the Flatiron Building on 23rd Street; a particularly windy spot where ladies' scandalous ankles were exposed by blown-up skirts.

signed a contract and made an agreement to sell certain services for certain amounts of time to your employer for a certain
amount of money. Suddenly, you're being used for other services
like babysitting your employer's kids, during times that are not
in your contract, for no money. Your employer isn't asking you to
do this because you made a fair deal, but purely because they're
calculating that you need this job and fear them enough to let
them rob you of your time for no pay. They'll smile and pretend
it's all well and good, and that you guys are "friends" or that this
is "networking," but they are stealing from you.

Normally, a book that claims to be from the Average Joe
point of view takes a pretty collectivist stance on these things.
Not us. Here's the attitude we want you to have the next time
your boss flips out about you not wanting to pick up their dry
cleaning:

"Actually, Boss, I understand every single part of 'pick
up your dry cleaning on Saturday,' I'd like to help you,
but I'm running a business here. What business? Me.
Remember, you contracted my business to do web development for you from 9 a.m. to 5 p.m., Monday through
Friday? At the specified location of your office, for an
annual lump sum paid out twelve times a year? With any
additional services to be rendered at an elevated hourly
rate, provided they are pertinent to the web development
you contracted me for? If you don't remember, no sweat,
I have a copy on file here and at my attorney's office. If
you'd like to negotiate a new contract to cover picking up
dry cleaning on Saturday, I'm sure we can discuss that on

Monday, when my business hours resume. Any attempt to void our current contract, however, will be interpreted as a hostile response to my business's refusal to perform services not included in said contract, and you will be hearing from our legal department. See you on Monday."

Obviously, this is an ideal. Saying this to your boss, unless you have Alec Baldwin–esque gravitas and certainty, is begging for a retaliatory response. It is this attitude, though, that we want to spread: that the contract between an employee and his employer is as inviolable as the contracts companies make between each other. Think of how much better work would be if what you agreed to when you shook your boss's hand in that job interview turned out to actually be true.

Bosses and would-be bosses alike all fancy themselves as lone capitalist heroes out of an Ayn Rand novel. What those self-absorbed objectivists forget is that Atlas was the only guy holding up the world. Sure, it mattered if he shrugged. In the real world if the private owner of a steel mill sells everything and moves to the mountains, the Communist Chinese buy it, break the union, and keep making steel. If all the steelworkers walked away then Atlas is pretty much fucked. This is why steelworkers are (were) good at unionizing.

In other industries it's tougher. Freelance graphic designers, for example, can't communicate among each other efficiently, so collective bargaining becomes impossible. You don't need a union, though, to stand up for everyone in your position, just like John Galt didn't need a union to stand up for millionaires worldwide. Work to make it so that anyone who caves to unreasonable demands is considered a scab, because every scab makes it harder for someone else to say no. Anyone who allows their boss to take advantage of them, or sees their boss doing it to someone else without saying something, is adding to the list of things you are expected to do for free for your boss and your job. If the airlines can charge us for carry-on luggage, we can sure as hell charge for driving four hours to pick up the VP's BlackBerry from the hooker's apartment where he left it.

"This is what business is, though. It sucks. It's work. We aren't supposed to like it, but it lets us feed our families. The system works." You know what else works? Monarchy. Aristocracy. Theocracy. Tyranny. Asbestos. All of them work; that doesn't mean they're good for us, or that there aren't superior replacements. That superior replacement starts here, with the PFM Revolution. Stand up, and through protest and prank and satire and strategy we will achieve respect for all who earn it in the workforce.

We've already given you hundreds of examples of what sucks and what to do about it. Before we go, we want to give you a little bit of hope. As we mentioned, we receive PFMs from the future, as well as from Tumblr. They arrive through the wormhole Ethernet from many possible near futures, but when we got these we knew that the Revolution had a real chance of success. Remember, these are not written in stone, but if you stand up and say "that's not what I'm paid to do!"—this could be your future:

> **Please fire me. My boss keeps giving me credit whenever I do his presentations for him, and now I get six calls a day from other departments and companies trying to get me to work there.**

Please fire me. I'm the only one in the office today because it rained and everyone else took the opportunity to telecommute. Now I'm left out of the video-conferencing fun.

Please fire me. My boss saw my status message about needing a babysitter for the weekend, and now my kids are going on a trip with her kids to Bermuda. I hope their annoying personalities don't rub off on my kids.

Please fire me. My boss is threatening me with a promotion, but I like my friends and responsibilities where I am!

Please fire me. I work in a restaurant, and the manager who used to make fun of me for wanting to be an actor just saw my first commercial and keeps telling the customers I'm a celebrity.

Please fire me. The CEO, CFO, and VP all took pay cuts so we could get the raises we were promised. We offered to get rid of our cafeteria food to keep the company jet, and they just laughed and showed us the new produce garden behind the office.

Please fire me. All anyone talks about is what their responsibilities are and how they can get them done on time. We're done work at 3 every day and then just nap for two hours because there's nothing left to discuss.

Please fire me. I work at an Apple store.

Please fire me. The guy in the cubicle next to mine is humming the theme song to *Mission Impossible* while banging on his drawers and cursing. It's almost like he wants me to go over there and scream at him . . . never mind he did. It was a surprise party.

Please fire me. My boss is only a year older than me and he just retired at forty-seven and handed over the keys. I don't know if I can handle this much money.

Revolutionary FAQs

Q: Can I get a position in the Revolution faster if my relatives are already members?

A: Your relatives have been fired for risk of contagious nepotism.

Acknowledgments

Please Fire Me. I helped get this franchise started and all I got was a lousy mention in the Acknowledgments.

The success of Please Fire Me has been such a huge surprise that I think I should first thank all the horrible bosses out there (not to mention the ones who actually have fired me) for creating an audience for our work. Then I should thank all the readers and posters of Please Fire Me—you deserve better at work and I hope we have made you laugh and perhaps given you some good direction in return for your stories.

The site would not exist at all if it were not for the versatile, hilarious, and inexhaustible Jill Morris. She has designed, moderated, edited, promoted, and written just about everything PFM since day two. You rock, and in a fair universe you would be a queen. And the book you are reading now would not exist if not for the comic genius of Johnny McNulty who came in at the eleventh hour (too late to get his name on the cover) and contributed some of the best material. Jill and Johnny will be writing the sequel and I hope they remember to mention me . . .

A special thanks goes out to Amy Pyle, our extraordinary editor, and her team at Kensington for doing such a fine job with this book; Jamel Oeser-Sweat and James Rothbart (legal eagles); Mischa Nachtigal (social network guru); Manny Amare and Duncan Crary (tech gurus); Trevor Laurence (AV tech); Brian Carter and Cara Petrus (illustrators); Melissa Gomez (photographer); Cheni Yerushalmi of Sunshine Suites (flexible office space); Jack Terricloth of World Inferno Friendship Society (musical inspiration); and Megan Hinds, James Howard Kunstler, Nancy Mauro and Samara O'Shea (early disciples).

Please Fire Me was inspired and heavily influenced by the New York storytelling scene, including David Ellis Dickerson (his book *House of Cards* is actually the parent of *PFM*); Sherry Weaver and her Speakeasy show; Seth Lind and his Told show; and storytellers Peter Aguero, Kevin Allison, Michele Carlo, Jennifer DeMeritt, Heidi Edsall, John Flynn, Faye Lane, Margot Leitman, Sarah Rainone, Adam Wade, Steve Zimmer, and Jeff Zimmerman.

On a personal note, I would like to thank my family and friends for their love and support, particularly Eleanor and Addison Chromy; Lucy and Bob Chromy; Ann, Rob, Emily, and Julie Cutajar; and Patrick Stenson. And finally above all, I would like to thank my muse and the one person that makes me believe all things are possible, Jamie Brenner.

—Adam Chromy

Please fire me. All my talented friends are too generous with their time and it's making me look bad.

First, thanks, of course, to Adam Chromy who came up with the brilliant idea to let people cry out "Please Fire Me!" and believed in me enough to run with it. Thanks to Ben Ragheb for helping me with design questions. The site led me to the wonderful experience of writing a book with him and the hilarious, prolific Johnny McNulty. Thank you to my parents Bruce and Charlotte Morris for allowing me to pursue my dreams of writing, and thanks to my friends for their support and laptops.

If you see a heavily detailed graphic, like the map in chapter 3, attribute the work to versatile comedian Ramsey Ess. And thanks to Eddie Brawley for letting me annoy him with Photo-Shop requests constantly for many, many weeks. Kristin Hillery, who used to be my editor and is a much better writer than me, deserves thanks for being available on such short notice with chapters 1 and 2. Big special thanks to Erik Tanouye; he helped punch up the manuscript with great jokes and helped focus our chapters. Finally, thank you to whoever I can find to proofread this before we send in the manuscript. Johnny? Great, thanks.

—Jill Morris

Other Thanks

Featured in photos with their permission. Yolanda Munov, Shyremia Latham, James Berry, Robert Shulman, Amber Nelson, Kelly Hudson, Don Fanelli, Alison Rich, Whitney Meers, David Bluvband, Sarah Claspell, Brynne McNulty, Kevin McNulty, Johnny McNulty, Arthur Meyer, Will Hines, Shannon

Coffey, Rob Michael Hugel, Julia Kwamya, Laura Willcox, Aaron Glaser, Jill Morris, Erik Tanouye, Ari Scott, Ellena Chmielewski, Jason Shabiro, Hal Phillips, Ben Ragheb, Bob Acevedo, Melanie Hamlett, Kirk Damato, Will Newman, Aaron Kheifets, Patrick Clair, Mike Scollins, Diana Kolsky, Emily Hoffman, Amey Goerlich, Zach Norton, Courtney Wielgus, Lisa Clark. Photos by Ari Scott. Extra thanks to Angela Lee of One Source Talent.

A Short Word About Johnny McNulty

Johnny McNulty is the silent but well-spoken co-author of *Please Fire Me.* He joined to help finish writing and producing the book. Despite all reasons to go to sleep and not prematurely lose hair, Johnny stayed up late and worked tirelessly through his exhaustion. He once wrote all night in the corner of the bathroom of a bed-and-breakfast while on vacation with his girlfriend. He organized the photo shoot, fought with legal for our parody of *Immortal Beloved* (and nobly lost), and through trial and error learned how to put together an art log of more than one hundred pictures. Without him the book would have been very different and suffered great joke casualties. Johnny is a prolific writer and wonderful comedian. We were extremely lucky to get to work with him, and his dedication to his craft is beyond admirable.

Johnny McNulty is a writer and comedian living in Brooklyn, New York. He is a performer at the Upright Citizens Brigade Theater in New York City, and a writer/performer for the Raspberry Brothers, a movie-mocking comedy troupe from Brooklyn. He has contributed freelance jokes to *SNL's* Weekend Update, the Onion, the Onion Sports Network, and the Onion News Network. His writings have also been seen on McSweeney's Internet Tendency, CollegeHumor.com and The DoppleGang.com Johnny graduated from the University of Pennsylvania in 2007 with a BA in Diplomatic History—the essential degree for any comedian. He'd like to thank his family and girlfriend for their patience in this process. He is on Facebook, because he exists.